Hollis L. Green

RECYCLED WORDS N' STUFF

A Collection Of Recycled Essays And Short Papers

GREEN WINE™
FAMILY BOOKS

RECYCLED WORDS N' STUFF
A Collection Of Recycled Essays
And Short Papers

Copyright © 2016 by Hollis L. Green

Library of Congress Control Number: 2016910081

Green, Hollis L., 1933 –

Recycled Words n' Stuff

ISBN 978-1-935434-86-3

Subject Codes and Description: 1: SOC039000 Social
Science: Sociology and Religion 2: REL077000 Religion: Faith 3:
REL116000 Religious Intolerance, Persecution, and Conflict

Cover design by Global Graphics

Printed in Australia, Brazil, France, Germany, Italy, Poland, Spain, UK,
and USA   Also available on Espresso Book Machine and anywhere good
books are sold.

The Press does not have ownership of the contents of a book; this is the
author's work and the author owns the copyright. All theory, concepts,
constructs, and perspectives are those of the author and not necessarily
the Press. They are presented for open and free discussion of the issues
involved. All comments and feedback should be directed to the Email:
[comments4author@aol.com] and the comments will be forwarded to the
author for response.

Order books from www.gea-books.com/bookstore/ or any place good
books are sold.

Published by

GreenWine Family Books™
A division of
GlobalEdAdvancePress
www.gea-books.com

This volume is dedicated to

My oldest son, Barton, who

Encouraged me to learn to use a

Computer and write down

Family stories so they would

Be preserved. Two-hundred and

Forty (240) such stories are

Published in my book

SO TALES.

Herein are other recycled

Words n' Stuff.

Recycled Words n' Stuff
A Collection of Recycled Essays & Short Papers

INDEX

AUTHOR'S PREFACE

An Explanation Of The Title

In an attempt to stretch her limited budget, my mother would buy day-old-bread, which she called "recycled bread." This is how the concept of "recycling" or "re-purposing" entered the family glossary. However, in this age of recycling most everything from garbage to literature is reused again and again. Through the years, when I repeated an anecdote or shared a story in conversation, my mother wanted to know if the story were true. She would ask, "Is that a so tale?" Significant events in my life and career are recycled here.

Some years ago I decided to follow the advice of a superannuated Minister who critiqued my early pulpit delivery. His name was R. P. Johnson, a pioneer preacher who sat patiently in each service and listened to my message. On Monday mornings, I would go by his home for a cup of coffee and listen to his assessment of my speaking. "Your basic problem, Brother Green, is that each time you speak you feel you must present something new that no one has ever thought of before." As a young man, having heard so many recycled sermons by pastors, I attempted to develop new material from my study. I was flabbergasted at his evaluation of my presentation of new and fresh material.

Sensing my frustration, he explained: "When the choir or a soloist learns a good song, they do not sing it once and discard it; each time the need arrives they sing it again. This is what you should do. When God gives you a message to meet a specific need, anytime that particular need exists, you may use the same material again." I began to understand about "spiritual recycling" and started to file away thoughts, ideas, topics, texts, etc. for later recycling. So this is where the notion for **RECYCLED WORDS N' STUFF** entered my awareness of sacred and reusable stuff.

As an academic committed to textbooks and research writing, anything less than a fully developed paragraph was out of my comfort zone. Recently, I saw two brief messages on bumper stickers that changed my appreciation for the "shorter version" of profound truths. The first bumper sticker declared, "If you are doing a work for God, you should have big plans" and the second, "If God is your copilot, change seats." The impact of these brief statements caused me to rethink my dependency on the full-length version of ideas.

As a published author of 50+ books, I have written on many subjects. Recently, I discovered material which preserved some of my early thoughts. In this collection of **RECYCLED WORDS N' STUFF**, are early thoughts, papers and items previously posted on Face Book, written as a Foreword, Preface, or Afterword, for other author's books, a collection of short narratives, and essays of general interest. Trust you are pleased with the selection of "stuff" scheduled for recycling. The episodes are in *random order* and are, hopefully, presented with ingenuity and verbal skill sufficient to evoke both humor and serious reflection.

Note: The scripture with EDNT following is from The EVERGREEN Devotional New Testament - ISBN 978-1-935434-26-9

RECYCLED WORDS N' STUFF

1. EVANGELISM THROUGH LIFESTYLE

Evangelism is a color word in Christianity: a divisive issue, but it was not so in New Testament times. It should not be today. Each group seems to have a different plan to save the world. Jesus left little room for multi-programming. His first recorded command "Let your light shine" and His last recorded instruction "You are to be witnesses," both point to the continuing assignment of believers to "make disciples" as they journey throughout the world. As Elton Trueblood once wrote, "A non-witnessing Christian is a contradiction in terms."

True believers must continue to advance the cause of Christ through lifestyle evangelism. With all the essential elements in place: the pastor functioning as a Called Servant; the laity in their full-pledged capacities to present Christ in the marketplace; the congregation in a central focus to support all missionary and evangelistic efforts; and the lost as the prime concern of all. This plan cannot be beaten as being New Testament – whether in the First or the Twenty-first century!

2. PERSONAL WEALTH AND KINGDOM ECONOMICS

The concept of personal "wealth" comes primarily from the sacred writings of the Old Testament.

> *A good man leaves an inheritance to his children's children: but the wealth of the wrongdoer is laid up for those who are well-grounded in faith.* (Proverbs 13:22 EDOT)

Under New Testament grace, divinely provided wealth is stored safely in the Kingdom Bank, where thieves cannot break in and steal, not in individual pockets or wallets.

> *He who is faithful in small things is trustworthy in big things. 11. If you have not been faithful in managing personal resources, who will trust you with true riches?* (Luke 16:10, 11 EDNT) *But we have this treasure in earthen vessels that the all-prevailing greatness of the power may be of God, and not from us.* (2 Corinthians 4:7 (EDNT) *For where your treasure is, there your heart will be also.* (Luke 12:34 EDNT)

God Supplies "Enough"

From personal experience it seems that regardless of individual income, the amount left is usually zero. The material system normally takes all the income of the poor. W. L. Prichard once shared with Mercer University students a simple plan for managing personal resources. Give the first-tenth to the Lord. Use the next eight-tenths for the obligations of life. Save the last-tenth and you will always have something for special gifts? Whoever follows this formula will have high satisfaction and the respect of both God and man. The concept and the word "wealth" is rarely used in the New Testament and normally means either "enough," "income," "purchase power," or funds required for living. See Acts 19:25 where Paul explains that *"...by this craft we have our livelihood."*

The "come back" Call to the Rich

It appears the rich have more than "enough" and should share their extra resources generously with the needy. This is the concept of paying it forward; not putting away for a rainy day or to accumulate personal wealth or to increase personal standing among peers. There is clear guidance from Jesus for those who have more than "enough" resources needed to support personal and family needs: share with the poor and follow Him. Jesus suggested that some had strayed from the right path and should take steps to follow the plan and "come back" to true discipleship.

> *One thing you lack: go sell your possessions and give the funds to the poor and you shall have treasure in heaven: and come back and follow Me. 22. And he was depressed at the request, and went away with great sadness: for he had much property. (And Jesus let him go!)* (Mark 10:21, 22 EDNT)

Gifts are Measured by the Cost to the Giver

Sacred Writings demonstrate that Jesus valued gifts in terms of the giver. Measuring totals and assessing the remainder seems to be the keys to understand the Divine perspective on the use of funds. Tithing, for example, is calculated by the amount of earned income; while gifts are valued by the amount remaining under individual control. The highest authority on the subject is Jesus as recorded in the Gospel of Mark:

> *41. And Jesus sat down in front of the collection-box, and observed the people dropping money into the chests: and many that were rich cast in much. 42. But one widow dropped in two copper coins out of her poverty, worth about a penny. 43. And Jesus called His disciples, saying I assure you, this poor widow has given more than all they who gave to the treasury: 44. For they all put in of their abundance; but she gave all she had, even all her living.* (Mark 12:41-44 EDNT)

A Word of Warning

The purpose of wealth is made clear in the writing of James. He observed that needed funds had long been kept from the poor and had become corroded. The gold and silver of the New Testament era was not pure and could corrode. Just as fine cloths stored improperly may become moth eaten and corrosion will damage or destroy stockpiled metal, so the hoarding of wealth dishonors the Divine plan for the use of material resources.

> *2. Corruption has fallen on your wealth and your fine clothes are food for moths. 3. Your gold and silver are corroded and made septic by rust; and the decay is proof to you of how worthless your coins are. It is a canker which will consume your family tree like fire. These are your last days and you spent them storing up a personal fortune for an undesirable outcome, 4. you have kept back the pay of the reapers who worked your land, and the great*

number of men in the Lord's army has heard
their cries against you. God listened to their
complaint. (James 5:2-4 EDNT)

The Starting Place

Wealth creation is not the starting place: the divine plan is to regularly share in giving, based on the ability of the giver. When one follows God's Plan, regardless of their financial position, valuable treasure is stored in Heaven's Bank and is available for Kingdom use. In reality it is Kingdom Wealth rather than earthly affluence that counts. However, true prosperity is to consider the "value" of personal funds from God's perspective, not by a monetary or budgetary perception. True wealth for participants in the Kingdom is their "purchasing power" based on divine evaluation of existing funds. For example: if the widow's mite had a higher coinage value than all the other gifts, then Kingdom Wealth should have more purchasing power for things needed to advance spiritual endeavors. Such value in reality is stored within a faith-based entity, not in the personal account of an individual. Believers share according to their ability and God multiplies their gifts to meet the needs of the Gospel. Obedience and sacrifice of believers builds wealth to advance the Kingdom of God!

Kingdom Economics

God intended that faith-based entities be supported and sustained by the moral and material interest of individual believers. God provides individuals with access to funds, and out of these Provisions of Providence, believers deposit into resources that advance Kingdom interests. The tithe is based on total earnings, but a gift is valued in terms of the giver. The widow's mite was measured by what she had left. Jesus assessed the gift of the widow as more valuable to the Kingdom than all the symbolic gifts of the wealthy because their gifts cost them almost nothing. All faith-based entities must see the small gifts of the poor as they are "valued by Jesus" and realize the purchase power of such gifts are not measured in monetary terms but by Kingdom value to the beneficiary. This is the way Kingdom economics work.

Believers Create Wealth for the Kingdom

Paul counseled the Corinthians to "abound in the grace of liberality." His example was the poor Macedonians who first gave themselves to God and then out of their deep poverty gave liberally to support the Gospel outreach. Consider the Scriptural method of giving: *without show* (Matthew 6:3); *regularly in proportion to personal assets* (1 Corinthians 16:2); *and liberally and cheerfully* (2 Corinthians 9:7).

Use of Kingdom Wealth

Faith-based leaders must be wise in the purchase of equipment and services. Unless they understand that their account stored in Heaven's Bank is for the advancement of the Gospel, they will normally spend more than is needed for things that do not advance the Gospel. When leaders calculate purchasing power only on the numerical value of coinage without considering the divinely added "wealth factor" based on the "sweat equity" of the giver and the divine multiplication factor, they waste Kingdom resources.

Energy Exchange

Voluntary labor for the Kingdom is a valuable asset for a faith-based entity. All believers are in "full-time" Christian service regardless of how they earn their living.

The faith-based lifestyle and service to God is not about money; it is about a personal connection with God and a sincere relationship to people. Christian workers are provided a stipend to be free to follow God's Call. When faith-based groups make service to God and outreach to the lost about money, they fail to understand the wealth stored in the Bank of Heaven that comes from the gifts of the poor: spiritual outreach is not about money; it is about obedience and people! Energy is exchanged for coinage. If one has money, labor can be secured to do the work. If one has no funds, they must exchange their energy (labor) for "enough" "income" to support their family and to do their share to advance the Good News of Grace. Little is much in God's sight!

A Little Boy's Lunch

The lunch of a little boy was "enough" for Jesus to feed 5,000 and have twelve baskets full left over. This is spiritual multiplication. Why can't we take the little we have and let God multiply it to sufficient levels to meet the needs of those around us? Submit what you have to God whether it is a penny or a pound, a gift or a talent, a song or poem; an essay or a book: God can use what you have to meet your needs and the needs of others. This is a hard lesson to learn, but a most valued lesson in the field of individual achievement and funding in faith-based endeavors.

Cattle of a 1,000 Hills

An old story about an individual short of funds was told to talk to God about the matter. Draw on your account in the Bank of Heaven and God may use a branch office near you. When you have more month than money, remember that God owns the cattle of a 1,000 hills and the gold in the hills! We must all permit God to handle our financial problems and the spiritual opportunities to share with others. This old proverb remains true, "Opportunity equals obligation!"

3. MAY DAY THOUGHTS

My thoughts on this MAY DAY! May 1 is a celebration of spring in many cultures, a National Holiday to celebrate worker's rights for some, but it has become a day of military bragging and political protest. I awoke this morning (May 1) with a memory of marching in MAY DAY PARADES in uniform to express my citizenship and the military might of America to influence world affairs. I had a fresh concern for my various roles in life and the incumbent obligations to those with whom I regularly associate.

My multiple roles in life are: an American Citizen, a Christian citizen of the world, a Husband to a faith-based partner, a Father of two sons, a Brother, an Uncle, a Cousin, a Minister, a Professor, and a Friend. Each of these roles provides certain positional authority to mentor and guide others with certain reservations and limitations.

As an **American Citizen**, I have certain rights and privileges not available to non-citizens. For example, only citizens have a right to express disapproval of the government or the actions of law abiding citizens or officials, this comes only to those who have and exercise the right to vote. Non-citizens, as guests in this country, do not have a voice to speak evil of others until they earn the right of citizenship and the obligation to vote. Those who enjoy citizenship and do not vote give up the right to a continued negative voice until the next election. Non-voting is considered negative participation and invalidates personal opposition to the direction and regulations of government. Of course, all citizens, whether they vote or not, have a right to protest and/or refuse to obey unjust laws and have the obligation to defend themselves and their family and property. Even this has limitations.

As a **Christian citizen** of the world, I have an obligation to express my true feelings and faith in a lifestyle witness to others, but do not have the right to censure or denounce others whose culture or belief system is different. It is the work of the Holy Spirit to "convict the world of righteousness, sin, and judgment" even though God may use individual moral and ethical lifestyle-witness to bring this about; it is God's work, not mine. I am to live my faith in a clear and self-sacrificial witness to others, love my enemies and pray for those who despitefully oppose Christian values. The clear witness is being a lifestyle example of faith-based values where "old things have passed away and all things have become new." This is the true re-incarnation of the spiritual self and the creation of light, life, and truth in belief and behavior. At first being Christian was a life-style recognized by others, afterword's, it became a mark of identification as a follower of Christ. (Acts 11:26)

As a **Husband**, I am to love and care for my God ordained partner in ministry.

As a **Father**, I am to care for and guide my own children first, before attempting to assist others with their family.

As a **Brother**, sharing the same gene pool with another, I am to demonstrate this special shared connectedness in every way possible. I am more related (kin) to a sibling, than to anyone else on the planet. This connection cannot be replicated or rejected. We are in the same boat, paddling in the same direction, going toward the same place, not just drifting downstream toward the great waterfall of neglect or rejection. These same facts relate to being an Uncle, Aunt or a Cousin. Such bloodline connections are neglected with great personal loss. Why, because they are supplied only by God. Broken relationships in gene pool connections should be reconciled at the earliest point in time.

As a **Minister**, I am limited to the broad parameters of Sacred Writings, not freed to espouse my rules or man-made doctrine or procedures. The New Testament must be rightly divided and the only guide to morality and behavior. There is no room for sectarian or partisan positions in sharing the basic news of salvation with the world.

As a **Professor**, I am given a special right by a student to express both sides of an argument or position and then permit the student to make up their mind as to their acceptance and use of the information. I do not have the right to demand or attempt to inforce my personal perception, only the duty to express my true understanding of an issue or a certain situation.

As a **Friend,** I am obligated to demonstrate an approachable and responsive attitude, be understanding and supportive of others, and provide advice or counsel only when requested or obviously required. Friendship is two people in the same ship, and it is not a battleship. Those who will not listen to sound guidance should be left alone. Unless one is willing to make corrections and/or changes, no amount of "talking to a deaf ear" will change things. It is never good to shorten the old adage to "Prayer changes things" when the full statement of wisdom was: "Prayer changes people and people change things!"

Well, so much for my personal expression and concerns for my faith, family, citizenship, professional obligations, and friendship. Perhaps it is good to think about such things. WHAT SAY YOU?

4. A TRAGIC CONCLUSION

Flying out of Rio de Janeiro, my seat mate was a young graduate student. Not often does a Protestant clergyman get to talk with an intellectual from Syria. I always value a cross-cultural conversation, so I looked forward to a learning experience.

A few minutes into the flight, I engaged the young man in conversation. "What are your goals in life?" I asked quietly. "I have but one goal. My life would be completely fulfilled if I could kill ten Israelis!" was his terse reply. He continued, "I would be willing to give my life in the process of completing that goal." At the moment, I could not think of a single person that was willing to die for their Christian convictions. That was a tragic conclusion!

In the light of the maltreatment of believers by those who freely declare destruction for Israel and America, how should we behave? The open opposition to Christianity in particular and Faith-based believers in general is increasing. The persecution happening overseas may well erupt on our shores. Then what will the faint of heart do? What will these do: the entitled generation, the complainers, the protesters, the non-voters, and those who oppose opposition to evil forces that would destroy the American way of life? Perhaps we should remember the words the German Pastor Martin Niemoller "...then they came for the Jews. And I didn't speak up because I wasn't a Jew...When they came for me, there was no one left to speak out." Maybe the words of a sword carrying Disciple, called Peter, would be appropriate here:

> *12. My dearly loved believers do not think the test by fire kindling about you is some strange thing happening only to you. 13. Rather rejoice when you share in some measure the sufferings of Christ; so leap and rejoice, triumph will be yours, when His glory is revealed. 14. If you are denounced for the sake of Christ, rejoice you are blood washed, for the strength of glory and the Spirit of God rests on you: 15. let it not be said that any of you underwent suffering as a murderer, or thief, or slander, or busybody; 16. but if a man is punished for being a Christian, he has no need to be ashamed; but let him bear that Christian name and bring glory to God. 17. **The time is ripe for judgment to begin with God's house: and if our turn comes first, what will be the end of those that disobey the gospel of God?** 18. And if the righteous are saved narrowly, what chance will the godless have? 19. Wherefore let those who suffer in accordance with the will of God, entrust their souls in well-doing to the Creator who is trustworthy and true. (1 Peter 4:12-19 EDNT)*

In your church family or among your professing friends, can you readily name one person who is willing to give his/her life for the cause of Christ? Look again at vs. *17. The time is ripe for judgment to begin with God's house:*

and if our turn comes first, what will be the end of those that disobey the gospel of God? Where do you stand? What is your solution to this difficulty?

5. MOTHER'S DAY MEMORIES

Sunday, May 8, 2016, was 20 Mother's Days without my mother. The pain of loss remains, but the memories are good. There is no replacement for a mother's love and concern. Perhaps we should attempt to develop such affection for others. Paul established and expressed such love for his converts:

> *"But we were tender among you, even as a nursing mother warmly takes pleasure in her children: 8. so affectionately longing for you, we were willing to share with you, not only the gospel of God, but also well-pleased to share our lives, because you were valued by us."* (1 Thessalonians 2:7, 8 EDNT)

Grace Irene Curton was born on the wintery morning of February 11, 1905, the third child of Ida Aldona Dobbs and Robert Tate Curton. She became a school teacher in Rhea Co. Tennessee, and a chance meeting made her the bride of Herbert Barton Green. Grace taught Sunday school most of her life and served as Dorm Mother for Nurses-in-Residence in Ohio and Pennsylvania, then served as Dorm Dean at Lee College before retiring at age 67. In her later life, she traveled extensively in the US, to the Caribbean, and four trips to Oxford, UK. On one occasion she brought back a suitcase full of books, when the Custom Agent lifted the heavy case and asked "What's in here?" Mother answered, "Books, I read a lot!" She read to keep her mind active and it worked.

In the early morning hours of May 4, 1996, she finally realized the truth of her long held philosophy: *"Never be afraid to trust your unknown future to the all-knowing God,"* and she once wrote, *"If God sends us on rocky ground, He prepares strong shoes."* After 91 years, two months and 22 days, the earthly life of Teacher Grace came to a close. As the mother of three and a widow of 59 years approached the threshold of reunion with Barton, she was alert and at peace. Her last words are not only a tribute to her life, they are a testimony of her faith; teaching those who remain the ultimate Lesson of Grace...*"I'm not afraid. I am ready to go."*

6. CRAMMING FOR THE FINAL

One day my Grandmother, Mattie Barton Green, (1883-1966), sat on the front porch rocking and reading the big family Bible. A grandchild asked her what she was doing. She responded, "Cramming for my final exams." Seeing Grandmother meditate and read the Bible was always a source of comfort for me. Grandparents have much more influence on their grandchildren than they ever realize. This influence works even after they are gone. Hardly a day passes that I don't remember something they said or did, especially the attention they gave me and their interest in my life and career. Grandparents are God's special gifts!

7. COPING WITH THE AGING PROCESS - IN RAP

[My first attempt at RAP]

"Speak sharply and swiftly"

QUESTION: What I gonna do?

What I gonna do, when I can't ask who?
What I gonna do, when I can't do?
What I gonna do, when I can't climb a tree?
What I gonna do, when I can't see?
What I gonna do, when I can't avoid strife?
What I gonna do, when I can't find my wife?
What I gonna do, when I can't eat meat?
What I gonna do, when I can't walk the street?
What I gonna do, when I can't shovel gravel?
What I gonna do, when I can't travel?
What I gonna do, when I can't count sheep?
What I gonna do, when I can't sleep?
What I gonna do, when I can't accept dares?
What I gonna do, when I can't climb stairs?
What I gonna do, when I can't stand up?
What I gonna do, when I can't get up?
What I gonna do, when I can't clearly see?
What I gonna do, when I can't use a PC?
What I gonna do, when I can't sleep at night?
What I gonna do, when I can't write?
What I gonna do, when I can't clear my head?
What I gonna do, when I can't go to bed?
What I gonna do, when I can't high five?
What I gonna do, when I can't drive?
What I gonna do, when I can't watch the news?
What I gonna do, when I can't tie my shoes?
What I gonna do, when I can't teach?
What I gonna do, when I can't preach?
What I gonna do, when I can't help cook?
What I gonna do, when I can't write books?
What I gonna do, when I can't be for hire?
What I gonna do, when I have to retire?
What I gonna do, when I can't tie my tie?
What I gonna do, when it's time to die?
What I gonna do, when they put me in the ground?
What I gonna do, when the trumpet sounds?
**ANSWER: Go to Heaven and enjoy eternal
life - forever!**

8. CANDY STICKS AND ORANGES

My father's oldest brother, William O. Green, (1903-1991), would invite my family to spend the Christmas Holidays with his family. For nine years after the death of my father, we spent the holidays with this loving and happy family. It was William's way to assist a beloved brother's family during the Season when Daddy was missed the most. Uncle William was poor by some standards, but his family had plenty to eat and there were lots of children with whom to play and plenty of things to do. I learned that family and caring for others makes one rich beyond measure. His wife, Edith Sparks Green, (1910-1991), was a good mother, a great cook, and always managed to make us feel both at home and loved.

One Christmas Eve I shall always remember. Looking out the window, I saw my uncle, who was a big man, carrying on his shoulder a crate and a box of something under his arm. I learned the crate contained oranges, and the box was filled with pepper-mint stick candy. He had bought it on credit and carried it three miles to make Christmas bright for all the children.

While we sat by the wood fire, Uncle William took out his pocket knife, cut a hole in an orange, stuck a peppermint stick in the hole, and passed it along until everyone had one. Then he showed us how to squeeze the orange and suck the juice through the porous candy stick. It made the juice so sweet and brightened the face of all the children. After all it was Christmas time!

With the fire burning warmly, sweet candy, oranges, and love, we always had a great Christmas. I often sit in the place where his house stood (It is now Green Oak's Park on the campus of Oxford Graduate School) and think of the days of peppermint sticks and oranges. They were the good ole days! I still enjoy peppermint and love to eat oranges because they remind me of my childhood and the Christmas Holidays at Uncle William's house.

9. FUNNY PAPER ON THE WALL

As a child I enjoyed my visits to Aunt Edith's, especially the overnight ones. She managed her house well on a small budget and kept everything clean. One of the ways she kept the walls clean was to paper them with newspaper. It also served as a form of insulation. The bedrooms where the children slept were often papered with the Sunday multiple colored funny papers. I enjoyed reading the comics on the wall and on the ceiling, too.

The site is now called Green Oaks Park. I pass it almost every day, and among other good memories, I think of the funny paper on the wall and Aunt Edith's cooking, especially during the holidays. Her tradition on Easter morning was to have a contest to see which child could eat the most eggs. I never did win, but I enjoyed the eating and the excitement. I always felt full on Easter morning and didn't want to eat eggs for several days.

10. BETTY'S PRAY AND PUSH

Pray and push as onward we go,
When is the end no one knows.
If you pray and push, it will be a treat,
As angels in Heaven know our every need.
They sometimes visit here on earth,
To let you know you are reaching your goal.

When we grow old, as life goes on,
We know pray and push is here to stay.
No one knows when our time is up
To meet our Maker we love so much.
Make me a blessing along the way,
For we are not here to stay.

So high and low we exalt our Lord;
He knows how hard we push.
So pray and pray and push and push
Till we meet our Maker.
If we don't knock, the door won't open,
So pray and pray and push until it opens.

Keep the faith and never give up!

My name is Betty Stout,
and I approve this message.
September 25, 2006

Betty was my older sister.

11. PREVIOUS PATTERNS OF BEHAVIOR

Tradition and a lazy approach to prayer and scriptural activity have permitted believers to become stuck in previous patterns of behavior. Believers attend church and feel as if they have done God a service. This attitude causes many to be stuck in the ways of the past with few creative ideas or individual initiatives in outreach to meet the needs of the community. The scriptural injunction is for present action in the field that is ready for harvest. The ways and means of the past may not inform the present needs of the lost. Worship and spiritual fellowship should generate the "force" to go forth and share the good news. What has happened to spiritual "outreach" by the congregation?

12. HOLY TELEVISION CAFE

A child was born in ancient Israel at the time the Ark of the Covenant was taken away and the child was named Ichabod meaning "The glory is departed." (1 Samuel 4:21) A sign over the door of a closed church was "ICHABOD" and appropriate because the glory was departed. Perhaps a secondary sign over the Church Kitchen, "Kitchen Closed – Cook on Strike" would inform the public. One might as well burn the holy cookbooks because all the old church folk are eating fast food specials at the Holy Television Cafe that serves up exotic and newfangled dishes. Oh, I forgot, the Holy Television Cafe has a framed pictures of Jesus (in color), a copy The Last Supper painting, a couple of old church stained-glass windows with images of Saints, and a large framed copy of the Ten Commandments on the wall. The folk who eat there regularly seem to have deep religious feelings. I understand they have specials on Sunday morning and Wednesday evening and serve a form of electronic communion. How could a meeting of family and friends become a gathering of strangers at an electronic feeding trough? Who would have believed it could be so?

13. OPPORTUNITY EQUALS OBLIGATION

I did not want to advance this issue until Muhammad Ali had been honored for his achievements in life. Watching the recent memorial ceremony, it appeared that Ali was a man of faith. Then I remembered the news a friend shared years ago. My friend, Lewis J. Willis, sat by Muhammad Ali on a flight out of Atlanta soon after the boxer converted to Islam and changed his name. Mr. Willis asked him why he made the switch from Christianity to Islam. His response was shocking.

"There was no challenge in Christianity; Islam gave me a way to change the world." Ali was confident in his statement, firm in his conviction, and satisfied with his decision. Who failed Cassias Clay? In his hour of glory he made a drastic switch from the teachings of his Christian Mother. Did someone fail to lead him to a personal experience with Christ? Who missed an opportunity to harness this strong voice for a spiritual witness?

The Christian faith provides a means to change individuals and the world.

> *Therefore, if any man be in Christ, he is a new creation: observe, the old things have passed away; all things have become new. (2 Corinthians 5:17 EDNT)*

True conversion works. Anything less is not valid Christianity. True believers can change the world one person and one day at a time. The big question, "How many other Mother's sons will slip through the cracks and become a spokes-person for another religion?" Christianity must compete for the minds, souls and hearts of the young in the marketplace to remain viable in the Twenty-first Century. What have you done recently to advance the Cause of Christ? Do you know a young person in your faith-based worship or community who needs guidance to become a disciple of Christ? Don't miss an opportunity to witness to God's saving grace. The old adage remains true, "Opportunity equals obligation."

14. CHARACTER OF THE FEW ATTRIBUTED
TO THE WHOLE

Reading to frame my thinking for the day, it dawned on me that little was learned from history. Being a young boy when WWII started, the wartime stories and the hatred they generated, always fascinated me. It appears that America followed the thinking of Winston Churchill when he "fused the Germans and the Nazis into a single hated enemy" in order to defeat a Nazis ideology that controlled Germany (1933-1945). The same was true of the Japanese: after Pearl Harbor most people were unable to separate the Japanese war machine from the people of Japan. Often the character and behavior of some within the culture is attributed to the whole. My question: "Are we doing the same with Islam?"

Could we separate the radical Jihadist Movement (the militants who pervert a religion) from the culture of the whole? Could we defuse the linkage of the terrorist activities of a few from a culture and still defeat the band of irregular soldiers who wish to destroy American values? It comes down to moral philosophy: how we ought to live our lives. Do we not remove a deadly cancer and the patient survives? ...of course, the Patient must agree to and cooperate with the procedure! Do you have any thoughts on this subject?

15. STAND TOGETHER AGAINST ALL VIOLENCE

Moral citizenship requires one to warn others of potential danger. If you see something, say something. Since there are no constitutional prohibitions to "Crying FIRE" in a crowded building, why do "citizens" feel reluctant to say something when they see a potential tragedy developing? The Constitution protects citizens right to gun ownership, but they do not have a right to collect guns and stock pile ammunition that threatens the community? Perhaps we should be reminded of the adage, "An ounce of prevention is worth a pound of cure." We must stand together against all violence aimed toward the unprotected. No one has the right to abuse or use the U. S. Constitution as "protection" while they plan acts of terror on the unprotected citizens of the United States of America.

16. FOUNDATION STONES OF OGS

At the inauguration of Dr. Kimberly Geiger as the 5th President of Oxford Graduate School; my words (Oxford Chapel 9/18/2015):

The best advice about my personal education came from Col. Bates, U.S. Army. Learning that I had decided to enter the Ministry and not make Military Service my career, he called me to his office. Looking straight at me, Col. Bates said, "Don't think you can go to school for 4, 5, 6 or 7 years and ever communicate with anyone. What you need to do is go to school part-time and work full time with people. You must stay in touch with the real world; do not get lost in academia." Out of this advice came my interest in interdisciplinary education that produced an alternative educational delivery system for mature professionals that we know today as Oxford Graduate School, OASI University, Alpha Institute of Ministry (AIM), Community And Family Education (C.A.F.E.), Accelerated Performance Training (APT), Yeshiva Torah Institute, and The Learning Centre.

This type of education provides the ability to view a subject or phenomenon through an integration of different disciplines and includes an effort to overcome sectarianism and freeze-frame thinking that hinders mutual acceptance among peoples, Faith-based groups, and generational or cultural exchanges.

Traveling for a decade in Europe and the British Empire with Associated Institution Developers, Ltd. (A.I.D.), a corporate development project provided an understanding of the English and the European educational systems. In 1974 a Task Force of 100 professionals was formed to work for seven years and decide how to best change the world in our life time. After considering many options, it was decided to emphasize social research and develop a global SOCIETY OF SCHOLARS and graduate programs for mature, social professionals. Why? It was determined that the other programs would take 20 to 30 years before an individual would develop the ability to make intentional lifestyle and professional changes to their immediate environment or become a world changer.

The Task Force decided to engage well-educated adults with an already determined professional orientation to influence positive social change through social scientific research. With the approval and assistance of the Tennessee Higher Education Commission, the Task Force following guidelines from the Carnegie Report on Higher Education concerning lifelong learning and research institutions, founded Oxford Graduate School in 1981 as a research institution appropriate for Christian scholars. Although the Founders had a multicultural Judeo-Christian heritage, they decided against structuring a school of theology, a divinity school, or a sectarian seminary.

The Task Force wanted to build a graduate school where Christian scholars would feel safe to think about academic issues and social change. General Jerry Curry, the Task Force Moderator, was asked to be the founding President, but the US Army extended his active duty and sent him to Europe; consequently, the burden of early leadership fell on others. The objectives were to put principles and values back into business and industry, integrate morality and ethics in society, and bring social scientific research to bear on community, family, and Faith-based entities. Busy professionals were recruited who wanted to advance their academic standing. We did not want people who just wanted a degree; we wanted mature individuals who wanted to change the world!

The intention was to develop a collaborative educational brokerage associated with multiple institutions through a Society of Scholars to build a delivery model that would reach individuals in the social professions. With a connection to three world-class libraries: the Library of Congress (DC), The British Library (London), and the Bodleian Library (Oxford, UK) and an operation in Oxford, UK known as the American Centre for Religion/Society Studies (ACRSS), the programs were developed and structured to operate as a "poor man's Rhodes project" to introduce advanced students to an American/ English model of reading, research, and learning. Task Force plans were freely discussed with key people at the University of Oxford who encouraged an American enterprise based on their history. Several of their top leadership were early Degree Day Speakers and encouraged this venture.

A strong social scientific research program was developed and during the next 20 years we recruited students from the USA and 32 countries and offered two masters and one European-style Doctor of Philosophy (DPhil) in the sociological integration of religion and society with an emphasis on social scientific research and social change using methodology accepted by state universities. Early OGS dissertations were evaluated by the University of Tennessee and the University of Oxford and judged defendable. University Microfilm published the dissertations for 12 years as a "research institution," until the word "Christian" was moved to make the statement read "Christian research institution appropriate for scholars." We learned that even small changes need to be carefully vetted. The Founders were guided by seven essential elements that characterized a nonsectarian institution structured to support social scientific research, global change and lifelong learning:

1. Establish a bridging framework to facilitate lifelong learning through elements of both traditional and distance education.

2. Negotiate partnerships and strategic associations with other institutions and Faith-based groups to insure positive social change through social research.

3. Facilitate interdisciplinary research of interest to the family, the community and Faith-based groups using methodology approved by quality universities.

4. Develop a teaching/learning process presented in integrative core sessions that permits self-directed learning in real life situations with lifelong learning strategies that used one's profession as a field laboratory.

5. Initiate academic policies and mechanisms to give priority to self-directed learning using assignments that extended for 30, 60, 90, and 120 days.

6. Establish professional, personal and electronic dialog/support systems suitable for faculty and mature adult learners.

7. Strive for a global strategy with a broad exchange
of teaching/learning systems and collaboration
across national boundaries to assure that graduates
became a significant force for global social change.

The rest is history! We are here today for the
inauguration of the fifth President/CEO of this institution.
Dr. Kimberly Geiger has proved herself worthy of
this position. May God grant her, the Board, Faculty,
Alumni, and Students the courage and strength to lead
this institution in fulfilling the spiritual and educational
commitments of the Founders? This is my prayer and the
purpose of this gathering. God bless you and God Bless the
future of Oxford Graduate School!

17. A WRITTEN RECORD

My firm conviction is that each believer
should record every blessing including answers to prayers.
If individuals would keep a written journal of God's dealing
with them, their family, friends and place of worship. Such
a journal would read much like a chapter in the Book of
Acts. An available record of God's intervention in their
personal lives, answered prayers, spiritual enablement for
special tasks, and the general working of the Holy Spirit in
their local church could become a great mainstay during
difficult times. If one could go to their own journal and be
reminded of God's blessings, it would create stamina to
continue through the normal difficulties of life. Memories
usually fade with time and a written record would refresh
the recollection of God's past blessings and encourage one
on their spiritual journey regardless of the difficulties. What
if we did not have the written record known as the Bible?

In this day of modern technology it seems that many have neglected a personal and systematic study of the Word as well as the benefits of personal devotional reading. The emptiness created from a life busy with doing "things" and seeking personal pleasure rather than using the calming comfort of prayer and the Word. Why did God preserve the written record of His dealing with mankind from the Creation to the Revelation of Jesus Christ and to the record of the pristine congregations in the New Testament? This was done for our benefit, but we have to avail ourselves of the written record. Of course reading the Bible should be mixed with prayer for a clear understanding and to assure personal life-application.

Believers should develop a new mindset and dedication that brings a commitment to self-discipline devotional study, prayer, worship attendance, and lifestyle witness. Devotional Bible study is a good start, because reading devotionally will prompt prayer, worship and a lifestyle of moral behavior. Here is a seven step plan:

1. Mediate a moment in prayer to clear the mind and then read with an honest desire to receive what God is saying.

2. Seek to receive what the Word clearly means and apply it to your life.

3. Study the passage (paragraph) prayerfully depending on the Holy Spirit to illuminate the true meaning and personal value.

4. Does the passage bring to mind any prayer concerns? Write down those concerns so they can be remembered.

5. Permit the Holy Spirit to guide you to bring your life into spiritual compliance with the Word.

6. Let the Word speak directly to you, your family, your work, and your life situation.

7. After reading the Word, pray for the Holy Spirit to use the Word in your life to ensure spiritual growth. Share what you have learned with someone, anyone who will listen. If there is no one around to hear, write a note, send an email, phone someone and share what you have learned.

Jesus in a parable shared how the seed of the Word could be so easily lost because the soil was not prepared or the seed was not watered. It was clear that the "seed" was the Word of God. Reading or listening is not enough unless the individual nourishes the truth learned from the reading.

> *5. A farmer went out to sow his seed: and as he sowed, some seeds fell beside the footpath; and it was walked on, and the birds consumed it. 6. And some fell on rocky ground; and as soon as it came up, it withered away, because it lacked moisture. 7. And some fell among prickly weeds; and the thistles sprang up with it, and choked it. 8. And other seeds fell on good ground, and sprang up, and produced fruit a hundredfold. And when he had said these things, he cried, He that has ears to hear let him listen.. (Luke 8: 5-8 EDNT)*

18. FAMILY GIVES US ROOTS AND WINGS.

"Meet often with family and friends for weeds soon choke an unused path."

Notwithstanding the aches and pains of aging, I have learned to stop using my wings and reflect on my roots. Knowing the struggle of ancestors and understanding their accomplishments as teachers, soldiers, doctors, lawyers, politicians, preachers, women of worth, uncles of accomplishments, the courage of cousins, and sibling's achievements made me proud of my personal and spiritual heritage. I have learned that life is less "what you do" and more "who you are." I have learned to never say "no" but say "Yes, but let me check my calendar." A most significant aspect of aging was learning that maturity and life-experience provide wisdom to mind my own business. I have also learned that the last 5-years of life should be the most important; it is what all the other days were about! What are your plans for the next 5-years? Do these plans include participation in the "kinship reunion" with family and friends?

Early in my memory of the REUNION, I recall saying to my Granddaddy, "I don't think I'm kin to all these people." His response was memorable, "There are five bunches in the family: the horse stealing bunch, the sheep stealing bunch, the pig stealing bunch, the chicken stealing bunch, and the bunch that hasn't been caught!" To this, I asked, "to which bunch do I belong?" He simply said, "The sheep stealing bunch." I didn't understand so he explained further. "You see, we have lots of preachers in our family history and when people from other churches came to their church, it was called "sheep stealing." I got the message, but have always wondered about that "bunch that hasn't been caught." Are they the ones who do not attend the FAMILY REUNION? Yes, we call it the GREEN REUNION, but it represents a much larger kinship group. Perhaps we should start calling it the GREEN "KINSHIP" REUNION. The grandchildren of A. L. P. Green and Mattie Barton are looking for the bunch that hasn't been attending the REUNION. If you know any of that "bunch" please pass this INVITATION to them. We want everyone in the "kinship group" to be present LAST Sunday of August each year. We will eat about 1:00 PM. Bring a dish to share.

Family is a link to the past and a bridge to the future. It is important to remember those who gave us "roots" and "wings" also, gave us a sense of duty. Many things are important in life, but the duty to family is the glue that holds a kinship group together. Each member must assume responsibility to teach the next generation about their "kinship" connection, heritage and family relatives.

A key effort to advance the family is the REUNION, where children can see the linkage with others. Family becomes a "brand" that identifies this kinship group. The "kinship group" is connected through marriage to many other family names; whether your background connection is Spillman, Burns, Hudson, Stout, Tyner, Alexander, Prentice, Ellis, Russell, Jordon, Morgan, McPherson, White, Rigsby, Nash, Riddle, Merrill, Rush, Fite, Anderson, Searcy, Hunter, Young, Leath, Cunningham, Bowman, Russell, Breedlove, Greer, Walker, Sullivan, Buttram, Hartman, Hamilton, Millard, Upchurch, Spivey, Gist, Hughes, Simpson, Sparks, Standifer, Brown, Curton, Fraley, Dunn, Pogue, Durham, Jones, Cummings or if your parents or grandparents were named William and Edith, Orpha Kate and Jim, Barton and Grace, L.V. and Ruth, Marie and Nick, Edward and Cecile, Henegar and Ethel, Mary Ella and Bud, Betty and Buster or Hiram and Lorene...we are all part of the same kinship group, we are in the bloodline of George Green and Judith Spillman. We are all family! Let's come together in a Reunion, the last Sunday August.

Family provides both identity and pride. Below you will find many more names in this "kinship," but we are all part of the same "family group" and should come together to remember our heritage. The master LINK was George Green (1751) and Judith Spillman; the connecting LINKS were Joshua Somerfield Green and Anne Alexander, William Alexander and Lydia Caroline McPherson, William Thompson Green and Emma Bowman, and Robert Milo Green and Lydia White. This kinship group included Alexander Little Page (Dock) and Attie Mattie Barton. This is our immediate "kinship group" this is our bloodline and marriage linked family, but the family now extends to names like Shimonaka, Lutz, Bawthenheimer, Vanderhoff, Higgenbothem + many more.   Where is this bunch?

Family must have roots to produce fruit. Even our BRIDGE to the kinship group, "A. L. P." and Mattie, has many family name identifications: Alexander, Little, Page, Barton, Sparks, Brown, Curton, Pogue, Standifer, Fraley, Dunn, Durham, Jones, and Cunningham. The names of the next generation are known as, Weir, Whitfield, Wieck, Henderson, Dickerson, Kuhn, Burger, Medlin, Stout, Lane, Faust, Fowler, Huffaker, Elsea, Fortien, Travis, Sharp, Strickland, DuFresne, Suttles, Coulter, Gossett, and Dillard.* The major LINKS to the past are about gone. All of the children of A. L. P. together with their spouses have passed with the exception of the wife of Henegar, Ethel Fraley Green (she was 100 on May 18, 2016). The REUNION will celebrate the past, the present, and hopefully, the future. Come and have a historic photo!

It is important to remain both attracted and attached to the extended family. The family is aging and others are too ill to attend a reunion. The William O. Green family recently lost Brian Edward Green, Paul Edward Green, Robert Carl "Bobby" Weir, Alta Jean Green Weir, and Jeffery Martin Chaffin. Marie's son, Charles Donald Pogue recently passed and Orpha Kate's surviving daughter, Frances Brown Martin is in a nursing home. Most of A. L. P.'s grandchildren are living longer, but enjoying life less because of aches and pains and we sure would enjoying seeing you at the reunion. Isn't it a shame the young do not realize the value of the kinship or family? Let's gather and enjoy fellowship and the sharing of meaningful memories. Kinship lines often disappear after four (4) generations, the Green Family is beginning the 9th generation since George Green was born in Maryland (1751) shortly after his family arrived from Sussex, England.

I realize the calendar is running on all of us. Do not wait till next year! Bring your children and grand-children to the "kinship" REUNION and let's work together to build a bridge to the future. Hopefully, all who attend can share a "meaningful memory" about family and the value of REUNION. A tree has as much growth in the roots as it does in the foliage and fruit bearing area. You must have roots to produce fruit! **REUNION is the "kinship connection!"**

19. GAIL'S TRIBUTE TO MOTHER

When my mother, Grace Curton Green, passed in 1996, Gail wrote this in her memory:

MOTHER - She was a lady.

Head held high, yet not so high she could not see the need of her only son.

No restrictions placed on him - released to live his life as best he could.

How proud she was of her boy; just pure unadulterated love.

She was a comfort.
Grace.... a fitting name don't you think?

20. HAWKS WON'T GET THE CHICKENS

One summer, my older sister, Betty, was staying with Grandmother Green and trying to get her to go somewhere. Grandmother said she couldn't go because the hawks might get her chickens. Misunderstanding or just not knowing the difference between a hawk and a hollyhock, my sister took a hoe and chopped down all of grandmother's beautiful hollyhock flowers.

Rushing in Betty exclaimed, "We can go now, the hawks won't get your chickens 'cause I cut them all down!" Grandmother's measured response to my sister's sincere effort was a lesson in patience with a child. She liked flowers, but she loved grandchildren more. I wish all parents and grandparents were as patient as Grandmother Green. The world and all the children would be much better. The adults would be happier, too!

21. BECOMING EXHAUSTED WITH FACE BOOK

Sorry, friends but I am becoming exhausted, even bored, with so much information from the same people on Face Book. Out of courtesy for others, individuals should limit their FB input to daily or weekly information. I am weary with multiple posts by the same people on the same day and multiple posts every day. I do not know if others feel the same way, but this is how I feel.

I use FB to keep in touch with some 2,000 friends... not to be informed about everything that happens in someone's life! Who cares what time you get up or go to bed? Do we need to know about your cat, dog, car, or house? Let's save FB for important news that we need to know. The overload just discourages busy people from following friends on FB. Perhaps, we should initiate a new FB called "Blabbermouth Book" for people who have nothing to do but gossip and share everything with everybody. Of course, I know about LinkedIn, but that is a business network, Face Book is for "friends" and pictures of family and grandchildren on your virtual and pretend wall. Yes, I know about "unfriending" and "unfollow" but then I could miss all the gossip, rumormongering, and blabbermouth stuff! What would my world be without it? What say you?

22. NOODLE POP, THE PIG

When my youngest sister was a small child, she encountered an albino piglet. My Aunt Margie had separated it for a pet. Margie named the piglet, "Noodle Pop." Aside from the small white pig running loose, my sister thought all the pigs were noodle pops, and all pigs were called by that endearing name. One day Noodle Pop was gone - not just gone, but he sent to the market. I don't know when, or if ever, my sister got over her reluctance to eat pork. She thought she might be eating little "Noodle Pop." Pets can be endearing to a child, and the loss of a pet is a real blow to the little understood dynamics of separation. Childhood pets are a good way to learn about separation and even death so the big surprises of life are not so traumatic.

23. TRIBUTE TO ETHEL FRALEY GREEN
On Her 100th Birthday
May 18, 2016

PUSHING 100
Dedicated to Aunt Ethel

PUSHING 100, life is a blast;
Believe my health is going to last.
PUSHING 100, many friends have gone;
But I am still holding my own.
PUSHING 100, although children are grown;
Glad to live in my own home.
PUSHING 100, husband was first to pass;
I am happy to be the last.
PUSHING 100, I have grown a little;
But it is all in the middle.
PUSHING 100, with doctor's visits and taking pills;
I don't have time to be ill.
PUSHING 100, I can't walk very far;
I prefer to ride in a car.
PUSHING 100, enjoying family and friends more;
Always delighted to hear a knock at the door.
PUSHING 100, the battle for eternal life is won;
But believe I will try for 101!

24. A SAFE PLACE TO THINK

[www.ogs.edu]

In 1974, one-hundred professionals were
selected for the Oxford Task Force (1974-1981) to determine
how best to change the world in their lifetime. After
considering many options, it was decided to initiate a

graduate program for mature, social professionals as a freestanding research institution appropriate for Christian scholars. The program was designed with two groups in mind: mature graduate students and working professionals who desired to continue their education and develop additional competency in their occupation by engaging in scholarly research. While the degree was from an American institution, the MLitt and DPhil degree designations established a link with the European approach to graduate studies and specified an alternative delivery system.

After a decade of academic relationship building with the University of Oxford (UK), Oxford/ACRSS (American Centre for Religion/Society Studies) submitted an application for Centre Accreditation. On January 16, 1992, the Secretary of the Delegacy of Local Examinations at the University of Oxford announced that the Delegates had approved the appointment of the institution as a Centre for Examinations. The name and number given were Oxford Graduate School #10101.

While maintaining similar requirements as other graduate programs, the graduate program is distinctive in five areas. (1) All credits are class-based and core sessions are concentrated at significant points during residency sessions to deliver a specialized curriculum. (2) Faculty direction was individualized to cope with the diverse needs of graduate students. (3) Students were provided interactive guidance in the development of a research direction. (4) Problem-solving scientific research is applied to a social profession or vocation, and (5) academic work demonstrated an integration of religion and society and was directed toward positive social change.

The development of the "American Oxford Concept" was based on four assumptions about graduate work. First, the academic program builds on the foundation of previous course work and is not a duplication of previous studies. Second, contact with faculty was structured to fit the academic needs of students, but is not a substitute for self-discipline in acquiring both content and competency in a specified curriculum. Third, campus courses are supported by faculty-generated full-length texts/syllabi and essential components presented in core sessions concentrated with some transactional distance elements to promote in-depth learning of a subject and an adequate application of knowledge. Fourth, graduate study encourages faculty and students to interact with the problems of the social professions through academic research in resolving critical problems with the eventual outcome having a beneficial impact on society.

The traditional characteristics of education have changed since Oxford Graduate School was chartered in 1981. The natural features of the education landscape seem to change almost daily. Procedures and methodology that were taboo yesterday are acceptable or even advanced today. The past criticism of the Old World tutorial method has turned into imitation as it is used with new technology to meet the tutoring needs of learners separated from the traditional classroom. These concepts are compatible with the original intent of the Oxford Task Force (1974-1981) that proposed the development of a research institution for mature adult learners and a system to enhance lifelong learning. The education process for adult learners was guided by these essential elements that characterize institutions structured to support lifelong education.

1. Establish a bridging framework to provide the contexts to facilitate lifelong learning.

2. Negotiate partnerships and strategic linkages with other institutions and groups.

3. Develop a teaching/learning process that permits self-directed learning in real life situations.

4. Initiate academic policies and mechanisms to give priority to learning.

5. Establish dialog/support systems suitable for adult learners and graduate research.

6. Strive for a global strategy with a broad exchange of teaching/learning systems and international collaboration.

7. Facilitate social research directed toward the solution of problems in the family, community, and faith-based entities.

During the past decades Oxford Graduate School has carved a niche in American higher education. The academic venture is fully accredited and alumni and students are active participants in positive social change endeavors around the world. The founders were not willing to follow a totally secular or sacred model, but were concerned about interdisciplinary education that created a program where students from multiple faith-based groups could have a safe place to think, study, and integrate the essential elements of morality and ethics into society through positive social change using social scientific research.

25. TEAR DOWN THESE WALLS

At the Brandenburg Gate, in the wall that separated East and West Germany, U. S. President Ronald

Reagan challenged the Soviet leader to tear down the Berlin Wall as an indication of transparency, restructuring and freedom. The Gate was a limited passageway between a divided people and Reagan's call was not only for free access, but the breaking down of the conflict-ridden wall. He not only wanted free an unhindered passage through this gate, but also, the removal of the problematical wall that separated the people from kindred and the art, music, literature, and the collective and intellectual culture of Germany.

The Repaired Partition -- Reagan was not the first to speak of tearing down a wall that divided people. At the death of Jesus, the curtain wall that partitioned the temple and limited access to the Holy Place was divided. This opened access to the Holy Place and provided incentive for those who were left out to become participants. It appears that this wall of partition was repaired and again imposed limited access to sacred places. In the twenty-first century there must be courage to tear down the walls that separate cultures and people from access to worship and a spiritual path. It is true that the harmful aspects of walls can be removed without bringing impairment to the culture.

Open access to Seekers -- Paul, a pristine sacred writer, was clear that the life and death of Jesus broke down the wall that separated Jews and the rest of the world. Since the earliest believers accepted Jesus as the Right Path or route to God, no one should be excluded by culture, language or tradition. John, the Revelator wrote that *"the eternal gospel was preached to those who dwell on the earth, and to every race, and tribe, and language, and people"* (Revelation 14:6 EDNT). The walls that separate people and hinder free access to both public worship and private witness must be broken down, because Jesus abolished the hostility and dissolved the partition between the sacred and the seekers. Since access was opened to God's promises, all should become fellow citizens with the saints, and belong to the Household of Faith. Early believers saw individual converts as stones building on the foundation of the Prophets that would become a completed building closely joined together and growing into a sacred temple in the Lord (Ephesians 2: 11-22 EDNT). What happened to that sacred temple made from the hard rock commitment of new believers? What happened to free access to spiritual truth unfiltered by human tradition and behavior passed down within a group or society?

People Joined Together -- The place and act of worship has many names. This book uses the term "faith-based" instead of synagogue, church, mosque, or temple. The author does not use the word "church" to mean a place of public worship connected to a sectarian group. It is used as a broad term for people joined together to advance a moral or religious cause; that is, a community of faith, a congregation, a spiritual fellowship, a gathered group for religious activities, or any organization or group intentionally connected to a faith-based cause. Christian places of worship, Mosques or Jewish Synagogues are all faith-based and are part of the faith equation that has a moral and ethical obligation to influence individuals, families, and society through a message of grace. The term "faith-based" came into English use almost half a century ago to describe any group, organization or function based on religious beliefs or charitable intentions. All organizations loosely associated with a religious or moral cause are considered part of the faith-based community.

These are the people who could tear down the walls of misunderstanding, hatred, prejudice and racism that blocks the message of grace from reaching the world. This book is directed to the leadership of such groups.

A Way Forward -- All true believers must work diligently to communicate the message of grace in terms easily understood by the next generation. The cultural walls that limit access to the Right Path must be weakened to give individuals a way forward. Who has the audacity to begin the process? Who will unlock the gates as a first step to full access? Who will take the hammer of courage and the chisel of truth and begin opening the walls that separate people of faith in order to construct a better world?

True believers were called to share their faith and have an acclaimed tribute at the end of life. *For you were called to give kind words to others and come to a well-spoken eulogy at the end.* (1 Peter 3:9 EDNT) True faith will find a way into the heart and life of those who hear the message of grace and desire to live a moral and ethical life and assure a well-spoken eulogy at the end because *The Lord is not slow concerning His promise as some count slowness; but is longsuffering to all, not wishing any to perish, but desiring all to take the way of repentance.* (2 Peter 3:9 EDNT)

One Path to the Gates of Heaven -- Cooperation leads to friendship and friendship generates fellowship and fellowship produces solidarity of purpose. Social and cultural differences will always exist in faith-based groups. Being "right" is not sufficient might to tear down the walls and bring redemption to the world. Rather, it is to point to the simplicity and power of faith and the need to emphasize common tenets that bring people together. The faith-based way of life should be a force to unite rather than a wall to divide. The human factor or cultural limitation should not be allowed to complicate the universal values of the faith-based agenda. All must seek to follow the one Right Path to gates of heaven.

Synergetic Course of Action -- All major monotheistic religions have elements of syncretism in their beliefs or history, yet adherents fail to admit this fact. The combining of different, often contradictory beliefs, becomes a major problem for faith-based people. To admit this religious syncretism would be to betray the purity of their present belief system. Followers do not see or do not want to know the facts about such blending of other beliefs and unrelated traditions. This happens when multiple religions exist in the same culture or a new religion is force on a population. Normally, this does not entirely succeed and the former beliefs and old practices continue. Syncretism is the opposite of a synergetic course of action this book advocates. Syncretism is a silent or almost unnoticed step in accepting foreign ideas while the synergetic process is a transparent strategy toward cooperation in a common cause.

Personal Action can make a Difference -- Synergetic cooperation is not to suggest that Judaism, Christianity, or Islam should make a fatal compromise of their religious integrity. Culture and tradition are social glue that holds religions together. Yet, compromise ("*together-promise*") agreement is a necessary part of the process. A lack of willingness to cooperate and work together among monotheistic believers is a major difficulty in building a unified force to bring civility and redemption to the population of the earth and hopefully restore a semblance of unity within the message of grace. Individual believers are a powerful force in this effort. Where organized religions cannot or will not function, personal action can make a difference and break down some of the barriers to personal cooperation in a global agenda that could strengthen the One Lord-One Faith message.

26. AN AMAZING DELIVERANCE

John Newton, master of a slave ship, encountered a divine emancipation he called his "great deliverance," after praying during a storm at sea (1748). Continuing in the slave trade after this experience, he began to change his attitude and slaves under his care were treated humanely. Yet this change was not sufficient to satisfy a changed heart. He returned home, became a minister in the Church of England and wrote many songs.

Social change comes slowly -- The John Newton story is of a changed man who delayed positive action. It took a long time for him to change an agenda and act appropriately. After his heart was changed, his mind developed in a spiritual direction, and eventually he was able to execute positive acts toward the people he had wronged. His words and music still speak volumes today for anyone who will listen. This provides hope that positive and constructive change will come. The question is "Where, when and with whom will it begin?" Try closing your eyes and humming the tune to Amazing Grace: it can change your life.

Individuals Can Change -- In social theory one learns that individuals change more rapidly than groups; groups faster than communities; communities easier than society. An affirmative attitude is needed to make a drastic difference, but legislation for groups of people is not the objective. Individuals are the persons who can change. Leadership is the ability to influence others to follow one toward stated objectives. It is influence that changes individuals and changed individuals are able to influence group change. Then, small groups with an altered mindset can change the communities of which they are apart. Eventually, society will feel the force of gradual positive change. When it is gradual change overtime, social change will be accepted and even embraced. Most prefer instant change, but social change is sequential and incremental overtime. Patience is required.

False Human Barriers to Social Progress

-- This hopeful anticipation is based on the social theory timetable, but it should be remembered that discrimination and slavery did not begin with the American Colonies or the Southern Confederacy. This inequity and bigotry began in the wicked hearts and money-oriented minds of civilized men around the world who chose to abandon moral values and merchandise in African slaves. Perceiving themselves to be superior, this racial discrimination and bigotry built legal fences and social walls creating false human barriers to social progress. Some remnants of discrimination remain that perpetuate roadblocks to shared human advancement. Yet there were converts.

Lincoln and Grant Must be Given Credit

-- Segregation in the United States began centuries ago before America was a Nation. In the decade of the 1860's, America fought a Civil War and President Lincoln signed the Emancipation Proclamation to free all in servitude. On March 30, 1870 the Fifteenth Amendment was ratified:

"The rights of citizens of the United States to vote shall not be denied or abridged by the United States or any State on account of race, color, or previous condition of servitude." The following day, May 31, 1870 President Ulysses S. Grant signed the first Enforcement Act that substantially secured the voting rights of freedmen. One year later, President Grant signed the Second Enforcement Act (1871) to protect black suffrage and targeted the activities of violent groups that resisted the progress. About five years later, President Grant signed the Civil Rights Act of 1875. This groundbreaking act prohibited segregation in various modes of public accommodations and transportation and discrimination in jury selection.

Action Unsurpassed in Presidential History -- President Grant's role in securing the full political equality of all Americans regardless of race is unsurpassed in presidential history. Even after the popular will overwhelmingly turned against the President's efforts to protect the political and civil rights of former slaves, Ulysses S. Grant refused to abandon his commitment to those for whose freedom he had fought. After he left office, the federal government allowed the South to enter a new era of segregation and disfranchisement. During this period, President Grant's efforts to protect the freedmen during Reconstruction were widely ridiculed and declared to be misguided. Such criticism, however, has crumbled in the face of history.

The Kennedy/Johnson Effort -- About 100 years later, despite President Kennedy's assassination (1963), his proposal culminated in the Civil Rights Act of 1964. President Lyndon Johnson is given credit for pushing the Civil Rights Act through Congress.   Progress has been

made with minorities in Cabinet positions and in elected
office across the nation. The Inauguration of Barak Obama
(January 20, 2009) as the 44th President of the United
States of America was a major step in removing the social
guilt of the American people.

A Footnote to History -- A footnote to this
historical event: it should be noted that Black Men received
the right to vote before Women did. Black men were
"symbolically" given the right to vote in 1870 with the 15th
amendment, but in reality most did not vote out of fear
and intimidation by the white establishment. Women on
the other hand gained the right to vote in 1920 with the
19th amendment. Difficulties with voter registration and
the use of a poll tax which was not lifted until 1964 with
the 24th amendment. The Voting Rights Act of 1975 finally
gave black men the free opportunity to vote. Could this be
the reason people turned to Candidate Obama instead of
Mrs. Clinton? Perhaps next someone will push for a woman
President. With patience and tolerance, conceivably within
a decade or two the United States of America will develop
a color blind society and begin to function as a melting pot
rather than a stew pot.

A Social Change Timetable -- Everyone is in a
hurry to make constructive changes, but reality must be
faced squarely. Haste makes waste. It takes as long to solve
a social problem as it took to create the problem in the first
place. Some gender, racial, ethnic, religious, and national
origin issues have been with society for hundreds of years.
Does this mean constructive change can never happen in
one lifetime? Of course, not! However, understanding
the social theory does assist the appreciation for the small
changes one sees and increases the tolerance for the gradual

improvements that are taking place. Is the change moving fast enough? Of course, not! Again, the process can be nudged a little, but it cannot be pushed beyond the norms of a social change timetable.

Constructive Social Change -- Constructive social change does not come easy. Community leaders must make a contextual analysis of the population by looking at every aspect of the community. When the people are viewed as a whole one sees a different picture than when community is broken down into parts: cultures, traditions, ethnic groups, business organizations, government personnel, religious institutions, social clubs, medical facilities, and institutions of learning. Separating a whole into parts assists leaders in determining the nature, proportion, function, and relationship of various aspects of the community in order to weave or knit together a new integrated entity that would demonstrate positive social change.

Affirmative Attitude Required -- A minority cannot protect itself against the violence imposed by discrimination, injustice, or prejudice. When choices are made on the basis of gender, race, religion, ethnic origin or lifestyle rather than on core values and character, little can be done without external forces coming to the rescue. Internal resistance only breeds more expressions of violence and prejudicial behavior. Only a willing majority can honestly protect the minority within a given community, honestly negotiate from strength and have the will to make changes to gain constructive progress. This is not done by laws, but by clear rejection of negative behavior on both sides of the issue and an honest adjustment of attitude.   What is needed is not only affirmative action, but an affirmative attitude. Everyone must be seen as a person of worth with a potential productive contribution to the community. Without this attitude, positive social change will never happen.

A Small Difference -- Civil Rights Laws and affirmative action made a small difference for some in the level of overt expressions of discrimination and injustice, but not in the core attitude of the majority. There are still those in the majority that either accept the whole and reject the part or accept the part and reject the whole. What is needed is an affirmative attitude toward all people. The articulation of an assenting approach to responsible change, lawful behavior, and the attitude of a good neighbor should come from a positive predisposition to behave responsibly.

A Natural Phenomenon -- Normally, a population will accept a minority, an ethnic group, or a social class into the community to the degree the group exists on the national scene. Since people gather in groups according to cultural orientation: food selection, clothing style, music appreciation, spoken language, family religion, political choice, and ethnic background, different groups must be recognized and viewed based on their function in the community. When a single group grows beyond the national norm in a given community, others begin to show favoritism and express prejudice.

Discrimination has a Life of its Own -- Discrimination at first is a natural occurrence, but as crime, loss of jobs, and negative personal encounters increase more disapproving feelings are expressed. It then begins to take on a life of its own and grows exponentially until violence beaks out. Laws, housing and school zoning, highway and street constructions or similar efforts to fence in a minority cannot stop the growing feelings of anger. Prejudice, bigotry, and narrow mindedness are normally learned in the home, not on the streets. The family unit is the key to understanding discrimination. It would be good if everyone could accept the family next door and across the street as part of the community. It would be great if whole families could communicate as the younger children do.

Internal Redirection of Attitudes -- This level of communication will not happen until there is an internal redirection of attitudes at home; it will not happen until parents and older siblings behave responsibly and become examples of good citizens. However, individuals cannot change by themselves. Normally, it takes an outside force such as, religion, community recreation, political fairness, or just plain good and honest behavior to affect such change. It may take a drastic readjustment of the psyche or redemption of the spirit to make a major adjustment to the subconscious attitude of the heart and generate a willingness to behave responsibly.

Limits of Normal Social Change -- Part of the problem is that minority groups have raised their expectations beyond the limits of normal social change. Also, some of the majority have either stuck their heads in the sand or dug their heels in the dirt. Higher levels of change would require a drastic and costly revolution such as the Civil War. Tolerance must be taught, demonstrated, and lived daily in the community to prepare for constructive change. Discrimination must be condemned and punished. Honesty and fairness must control all relationships. Then, an only then, can a pluralistic community live in peace and comfort with neighbors at the family table next door or across the street. It is coming; be patient.

A Forgiving Spirit -- Patience is a virtue in social change. It is the ability to remain under pressure with a positive attitude until relief comes. That is why the Ancient Greeks called the sick folk who came to see a physician "patients," because they had to remain under the pressure of illness until the medical practitioner was able to treat the infirmity. Patience means a calm endurance of hardship, inconvenience or delay until better conditions arrive. Patience is identified by tolerance of a situation that is unacceptable; it is developed by misfortune and suffering, strengthened by enduring the present, magnified by uncomplaining hope, and characterized by a forgiving spirit directed toward those who resist change.

Roadblocks -- Some members of the minority have personally risen above the fray and been assisted over the wall and through the maze to a better life, but some individuals in minorities have been hindered in their personal and social progress. Some of the roadblocks have been within conservative politics, the religious community, inside community leadership, and sometimes within the minority itself. Some said Sunday morning was the most segregated hour of the week in America. Perhaps this is true, but is it by coercion or choice? When social integration works in education, housing, and the work place, why is Sunday morning still segregated? Could it be by choice based on cultural (Black) heritage?

One of my graduate students at Oxford Graduate School did a study to determine the impact of social integration on the survival of Southern Black Community-based organizations. When three indices were compared (Social Integration Index, Black Community-based organization Participation Index, and Black Heritage

Index), the level of social integration made no difference in community-based organization participation. Only the Black Heritage Index made a significant difference. The higher the Black Heritage Index the greater the probability of participation in ethnic-based worship. It was not segregation, but cultural heritage that drew them to the religious activities and the music that fulfilled their cultural needs.

So it is possible for a minority group to be integrated socially, economically, and educationally and still maintain ethnic-based activities. After all most of the local community-based organizations and all the denominations in America have a cultural control indicator. This is not a justification for Sunday segregation, but an explanation of how it has happened. In fact it is the minorities who continue this participation as part of a cultural and heritage expression. As long as ethnicity survives there will be ethnic-based activities. This will gradually change overtime, but it will change on its own, not by external forces or even gentle persuasion.

Integrated into the Social Fabric -- As the essential elements of personal faith, not sectarian dogma, are integrated into the social fabric of a community, there will be gradual social change. Only a drastic transformation of the heart or a spiritual renewal of the soul could speed up the process. Heritage and tradition are big components of social resistance to change. Heritage becomes a legacy passed on by tradition to the next generation. At times it may be perpetuated by inheritance factors when family elders have traditionally been associated with a particular institution or ethnic-based activity/experience, the young may feel obligated or privileged to follow the same path.

Most want to hold on to the memories and the subconscious imprinting of the past. The more this difficulty is understood, the better society will be in accepting the gradual social change that is predictable.

Sectarian Positions -- A cultural framework for establishing sectarian positions has been the norm in Christianity. Some American groups developed congregations out of the historical and cultural conditions of the American scene. The congregations of the (Christian) Restoration Movement and such groups as the Holiness and Pentecostal Movements are examples. It seems that cultural foundations can identify most, if not all American denominational groups. These cultural and regional origins have colored various interpretations of Scripture and transformed tradition into cultural barriers. Over time these various interpretations of sectarian teachings were given brand names and promoted as the correct and proper way to worship and find peace, happiness, and eternal life.

Cultural Roots or National Origins -- Most religious groups and divisions can be traced to cultural roots or national origins. The Roman Catholic identity is obvious. The Community-based organization of England, the Greek and Russian Orthodox Churches have obvious national influence. Methodist and Episcopal congregations have English beginnings, Presbyterians have Scottish roots, Lutherans have foundations in Germany, Baptists have European beginnings, and the list goes on. At one time in America, there was even a Swedish Baptist Church. This particular group changed its identity when it ran out of Swedes. American religious groups have created congregations clustered around sectarian constructs with brand names that have identified and advanced a particular perspective as an accurate interpretation of scripture. When the young are taught these traditions, it is difficult to make meaningful change or produce a spirit of cooperation among the various divisions in the community of faith.

Cultural Glasses -- Scripture, which is supposed to be the Word of God for all people, has been viewed through cultural glasses and the private interpretations differ from group to group. Consequently, universal truth became the exclusive domain of a particular religious authority and limited to a selected doctrinal or sectarian constituency. Various teachings and different doctrine were culturally interpreted but firmly and authoritatively proclaimed as the true and proper expression of the inspired scriptural writings. While Judaism, the Roman Catholics, and members of Islam have differences, a unified message is presented to the world. The Christian community accentuates differences as a badge of honor. Each group behaving as if they have found the "Holy Grail" and have exclusive access to the "secrets" of faith and practice. This facilitates the religious segregation in America and encourages division within families and communities.

American Judaism has small internal differences, but the Jewish community maintains a unified identity. When individuals are identified as being Jewish, one immediately has an idea of their basic values. Judaism has a sense of community and commitment to the individual and family. The public understands much of the essential elements of Jewish worship and family values.

Although some differences exist among Roman Catholics, they manage to present a unified voice to the average American citizen. Other sectarian groups, such as Mormons, Jehovah Witnesses, or Islam manage to overcome differences and present a common identity. This is not true of most Protestant communions in America. This greatly complicates the integration of moral principles into society. "Can two walk together except they agree?" Some of these basic moral principles and religious experiences would enhance the acceptance among minorities and greatly advance caring for one's neighbor and loving one another in true acts of common humanity, but human nature perpetuates division and conflict. No wonder the American church is failing to reach the next generation.

Identified and Branded -- American Protestants are not presently identified as "Christian," but as Baptist, Methodist, Lutheran, Pentecostal, Presbyterian, and the list goes on and on. This has become name-brand religion in the eyes of the community. As if this were not enough division, multiple identities and doctrines exist within each of these sectarian groups. Is this a result of the pluralism in America, and an inevitable consequence of an immigrant nation? Can American Christians not lay aside small traditional differences and develop a unified identity around common tenets? Are there no converts to the Christian Faith, just adherents to sectarian dogma? Must each individual who embraces a community of faith be branded and identified as free-range cattle belonging to a particular ranch or rancher? Must one belong to a particular political party to favor positive social change?

These differences are based on culture, tradition, and language, not on firm spiritual or exegetical grounds. Most scholars know these facts, but the community is turned off by the confused and muddled message. Constructive change is possible, but to affect such change there must be true change of heart and the lessening of sectarian dogma.

There must be more than an intellectual apprehension of facts; there must be acceptance of truth that can change hearts and lives. Otherwise, religion will have less influence on the community in the Twenty-first Century than in the past and communities will remain divided, segregated, separated, isolated, and not relevant to the present generation.

A Stained-Glass Barrier -- Sectarian groups meetings on Sunday have created a stained-glass barrier between the community and between religious groups with almost sameness of belief. Small cultural and traditional procedures continue to separate religious groups into a kind of franchise system. These divisions have become a barrier to the larger social integration of the community. These divisions became the building blocks of a cultural and communication barrier between the sacred and the secular communities. Some sectarian groups are not willing to alter religious vocabulary to understandable terms for the general public; consequently, they become a barrier to social change.

Freeze-Frame Thinking -- Early religious gatherings did not have a bound, printed document to argue over the parsing of Greek words or disagree over the grammatical description of a word or group of words. The early believers had an experiential relationship with a Person and enjoyed genuine fellowship with each other. The Bible is a relational book and is filled with attitudes to be caught, rather than doctrines to be taught. If these attitudes were practiced, leaders would discard name-brand religion that confuses society and freeze frame theology that divides the groups. Without agreement they cannot walk on the same path. If the churches were together on the little issues, perhaps Christians could get together on the big issue of segregation, justice, and discrimination. This freeze frame thinking has created a barrier to contemporary morality and values. Since constructive social change and integration take place at the level of ideas and values, ideology is the common ground of application and integration of the moral and ethical mindset in society. What is your mindset?

What are you willing to do? Most Christians have forgotten that it was a man of Africa, Simon of Cyrene, a passerby who was compelled by Roman Soldiers to carry the Cross of Jesus up to the place of Crucifixion on Calvary. Simon had two sons, Alexander and Rufus (Mark 15.21). They became leaders in the church. Some have forgotten that Dr. Martin Luther King, Jr. bravely carried the Civil Rights cross up the American Hill of Difficulty to his own death. His children have continued the struggle. What are you willing to do to make a difference in your community? Will you help someone carry their cross? Will you stand firm for the rights of others? One man - one vote can make a difference!

27. A THREE-SIDED PROBLEM -- At-risk Youth

Dealing with at-risk youth is a three-sided problem. When one attempts to unlock the antecedent cause and anticipate remedial action to prevent and rehabilitate at-risk youth, the problem becomes almost unsolvable. This three-sided difficulty must be separated into the past, present, and the future. Each aspect of the difficulty must be reviewed and evaluated based on a realistic intake assessment of the present situation of the client. Mentoring can only deal with the rehab aspects of the difficulty. Prevention is a whole other can of worms and the future is in the Hands of the Almighty. The individuals and circumstances that created the problem in the first place must be addressed by others. Since the old adage, "An ounce of prevention is worth a pound of cure" is true, a big question is obvious: why were the prevention steps not taken?

A Gigantic Task -- Unlocking the future for an at-risk youth is a gigantic task, but it must be tackled, confronted, endured, in the same way one would climb a difficult hill, weather a great storm, or eat an elephant (one bite at a time). Why is this difficult process necessary? It is perhaps the last best change to give the young person, and society, the possibility for a better future. Youth mentoring starts with the present, but must deal with the past and the future.

Painstaking Patience and Endurance -- Mentoring deals with an intake "snapshot" of the at-risk person and frames it in three dimensions of time and space: past, present, and future. The hard part begins when the Mentor attempts to make minor adjustments to the initial "snapshot" image. There are no computer programs with an automatic correction button. Painstaking patience and endurance on the part of both the Mentor and the Mentee must occur over time to move the process forward and understand the portrait in the context of the present state of the young person. There are only a few tools in the Mentor's snapshot correction box. These tools work best when the Mentor has sufficient background data to understand how the past experiences inform the present state. Background data enables the creation of a future portrait as to how the Mentee would look at the end of the mentoring process. This would be a composite and an idyllic portrayal of a young person facing the future with hope and confidence. How would this process work?

A Mental Snapshot -- After reviewing intake data about the past and a present interview with the client to create a mental snapshot of the Mentee, the Mentor would begin making corrections and alterations to the intake snapshot. Attempts at red face removal to eliminate the shame and embarrassment of being subjected to counseling and mentoring are the first steps. Then the Mentor would compare and contrast the real life situation of the at-risk client with an ideal or textbook case of mature young people who are well-adjusted emotionally and socially. At this point the Mentor may try enlarging the picture, then a little rotation to give a different perspective and finally some cropping of the snapshot to find the hidden elements that could be enlarged into a more mature lifestyle for the young person.

A Trial and Error Process -- The process may be trial and error but the procedures cannot be freeze framed into a one-size-fits-all strategy. The mentoring process remains one-on-one and each case is different. The Mentor is always searching for a composite picture for the future that resembles the young person. The resemblance must be sufficient for the client to easily identify with the composite image. When the client begins to see the possibility of becoming the person described in the portrait by the Mentor, the work of mentoring is on track to provide the young person with a hopeful future.

An Over Simplification -- Parenting and the home environment are normally blamed for the troubles experienced by young people. This is an over simplification. The record demonstrates that good parents can have troubled children. Also, it is obvious that good children often come from less than perfect parenting and schooling. The community, the school, the 24/7 media, the Internet, drugs and the criminal element share the blame with the environment. The issue is not whom society will blame, but how can the circumstances be altered that put young people at-risk? Perhaps a start in the right direction would be better parenting, better diets, better schools, better communities, more discipline, more adult interest in education, more jobs for young people, less exposure to the sexual revolution, less crime and violence, less exposure to drugs and the criminal element, and certainly less TV watching, less cell phone use, and less Internet surfing. Perhaps more faith-based teaching could be a factor in changing the environment.

Part of the Solution -- This effort is part of the solution. It is based on academic research and a structured analysis of the at-risk young people that culminated in a National Mentoring Program. In 2007 following a Public Consultations on Crime, it was recommended that a structured program be launched whereby trained personnel would provide one-on-one mentoring to youth-at–risk. A government leader's advisory, by Cabinet minute established an Inter-Ministerial Committee comprising five (5) stakeholder Ministries to develop a Structured Mentoring Program for Youth-at-Risk in Trinidad and Tobago. The program is under the auspices of the Ministry of National Security, other Ministries involved are: People and Social Development; Education; Sports and Youth Affairs; Science; Technology; and Tertiary Education.

In 2011, Joanne Spence-Baptiste, as a consultant to the Ministry of National Security, presented a draft

Operational Manual and other materials for government approval. The purpose of the material was to provide a common framework, based on best practice principles in support of a National Mentorship Program.

What Works Here could Work Elsewhere -- Trinidad and Tobago appears to be a microcosm of the Caribbean region and a functioning example of a small nation. It is assumed that a National Mentorship Program that works here would probably work elsewhere. This developing nation has a diverse population and a mix of ethnicity, religion, cultural and social strata, together with communication technology that links to global and geo-political alliances. This has impacted the structure, attitude, and performance of primary units of socialization resulting in a breakdown of families, morality, and spiritual values. All this has produced underachieving young people and the antecedents to youth becoming at-risk.

Part of the Rationale -- Both the opportunity and challenges became part of the rationale for this book. The underlying justification for the book came from an increase in single parenting, decrease in extended family networks, and technological innovations. It became clear that the family and the community, normally the providers of social capital, no longer were able to provide the necessary support for a growing youth population. The mentoring program was designed to act as a support system to at-risk young people who experience these challenges. Consequently, the focus of the mentoring program included dropout prevention, job training, school retention, basic literacy, community development, as well as the prevention of substance abuse, teen pregnancy and violence and crime. The basic objective is to develop a mentoring program where the Mentor becomes both a friend and role model to support and encourage the Mentee in holistic development.

Research and National Consultancy Available -- The author of the research that established the basis for the National Mentorship Program in Trinidad and Tobago is available to assist other nations in the greater Caribbean region. She and her staff would be privileged to assist other entities in the region in establishing a National Mentoring Initiative. Having served as a consultant to the Ministry of National Security in structuring the national mentoring policy, the author is available to governments, corporations, and private efforts to consult on the matter of initiating a mentoring effort. This consultancy is to provide a common framework, based on best practice principles to support and inform the design and development of a National Mentorship Policy. Literature and programmatic tools are available; such as, brochures, operational manuals, and promotional pieces to meet the needs of clients.

28. A LESSON FROM LITTLE LEAGUE

In VBS one summer the children were singing, "If you are saved and you know it, say AMEN!" One little blonde girl was singing, "If you are SAFE, etc." The teacher attempted to correct the child, but with no success. Her brother was a star in the Little League, and she understood "safe." She had never been lost and didn't understand the concept of being "saved." Later while preparing a Sunday sermon, I discovered the word "saved" meant "to make safe." Perhaps the little girl was correct; she was happy because she felt "safe." From the mouth of a child came a lesson learned, not in Sunday school or church, but from the Little League. Early sports participation has real value for all members of the family, especially the younger siblings of the ones on the team.

29. LESS BIASED FRAMEWORK

My fifty-year attempt to support Christianity at the congregational level required a generic blindness to the sectarian nature of American Christianity. This journey provided a less biased framework for social research related to the barriers caused by the clustering of churches into sectarian denominations. The effort to understand the church as a social institution and develop an appreciation for my religious heritage enhanced my personal Christian life and provided a basis for continued research, but brought concern related to the unholy desire to grow until a particular church is the largest in the geographic area.

Knowing that there were limitations to all growth, the mystery became how large could a gathered church could grow until the natural limitations and detrimental forces begin to operate against the watch care of the people. Would paid staff with specific job descriptions replace the heart and soul of pastoral ministry? Would individual needs get the same attention they had received in the church were family and friends were present?

Another concern was how large can such a program become until it ceases to be a true church with adequate watch care for all the people. Would such a large group become either a club for saints, or a kind of Super-Mart of religion? Would such unnatural growth bring about the disintegration of small community churches served by hardworking and caring men with the assistance of unpaid lay leadership who performed sufficient watch care over the congregation and the community? Would this effective instrument of community life and service to families become redundant as members flocked to be lost in the crowd of some super-church? These questions have not been answered, but some observations, assumptions, and conclusions have initiated the writing of this book.

Search for Antecedent Causes -- My search for antecedent causes for Protestant divisions has taken me into every region of the United States and required extensive travel in twenty-six countries.   Research was directed toward the social and cultural foundations of Protestant denominations. The problem of negative participation in the worship and educational programs of small community congregations has created declining attendance, as well as the destructive aspects of personal mental reservation to commitment and cognitive dissent to basic doctrines of Christianity.

In an effort to understand the sectarian view, extensive research was done on the oldest American Pentecostal denomination and the largest American Protestant group. Doctorates in Theology and in Philosophy were earned during this research. Meanwhile, my schedule has been filled with academic research and writing, but colleagues and friends have encouraged sequels to my best known works in this genre; <u>Why Churches Die</u>, <u>Why Wait Till Sunday?</u>, <u>Why Christianity Fails in America</u>, <u>Titanic Lessons</u>, <u>Fighting The Amalekites,</u> and <u>Tear Down These Walls</u> are a partial fulfillment of this effort related to church growth.

Research was directed toward the social and cultural foundations of American denominations. The problem of negative participation in the ministry of American congregations has created declining attendance, as well as the destructive aspects of personal mental reservation to commitment and cognitive dissent to doctrine. In an effort to understand the sectarian view, extensive research was done on the oldest American Pentecostal denomination and the largest American Protestant group. Doctorates in Theology, Philosophy, and Education were earned during this search. Meanwhile, my schedule was filled with academic research and writing.

Over the years this research has been reported in various books. <u>Hitching your Star to a Wagon</u> (1958) <u>Dynamics of Christian Discipleship</u> (1962) dealt with the individual and personal nature of the Christian life. <u>Christian Education Cyclopedia</u> (1965) was an effort to preserve workable programs and methods for faith-based education, <u>Marching As To War(1969)</u> was a church history text. <u>Understanding Pentecostalism</u> (1970) was an effort to grasp the influence of doctrine on individual laity and understand what was happening on the American scene. <u>Why Churches Die (1972)</u> presented the difficulties of operating the church as a social institution or business organization without spiritual foundation. <u>Why Wait Till Sunday? (1975)</u> suggested a plan for renewal of a weak congregation troubled by the "human element" and the problem of "upward delegation."

<u>Understanding Scientific Research</u> (1982) was a social scientific research text for the social professions in an effort to get others involved in research related to morality and ethics in business and industry, principles and values in the professions, and the sociological integration of religion into society. <u>Sympathetic Leadership Cybernetics</u> (2007) a guide to serving the needs of people through shepherd

management and servant leadership. <u>Interpreting an Author's Words</u> (2008) refined study and writing skills by understanding how to interpret the written words of others. <u>Titanic Lessons</u> (2008) an answer to the question: "Do historic realities predict problems for a growing faith-based group?" <u>Fighting the Amalekites</u> (2008) a treatise on spiritual warfare. <u>Remedial and Surrogate Parenting</u> (2009) presented parenting skills as an essential aspect of faith-based lifestyle. <u>Why Christianity Fails in America</u> (2010) was a call for an internal redirection of the heart and soul to make Christianity viable in the Twenty-first century. <u>How to Build a Better Spouse Trap (2010)</u> how to break the cycle of dysfunctional relationships and make marriage and family an essential part of faith-based behavior.

Through the years a dozen Children's Novellas have been produced, namely: *Sleepy Town Lullaby and Story; The Funky Chicken's Wedding; The Scoop about Birthday Soup; Cranky Not-so-Hottra' Cat- Astropic Charlie; A Tea Party at Nany's House; The Shimonaka Big Dripper; The Mouse of the House; The Boy Who Wanted to Grow a Beard; The Trouble with Funny Book Cussing; The Blue Jay and Grandma's Song; and Ditala Killed a Dead Snake.*

"***Books adults enjoy reading to children and children enjoy again and again***"

<u>So Tales</u> (2011) preserving true stories for the benefit of family and friends. <u>Designing Valid Research</u> (2011) guidance for students to produce social research supported by tested hypotheses. <u>The EVERGREEN Devotional New Testament—Complete</u> Edition (2013) a 42-year project to translate common NT Greek into a devotional language. <u>Transformational Leadership in Education</u> (2013) a strengths-based approach to education.

Tear Down These Walls (2013) a priority agenda to make people moral citizens of the world before they can become mystical citizens of heaven. Research Methods for Problem Solvers and Critical Thinkers (2016) guidance for students in tertiary education to develop theses and dissertations in the social sciences dealing with positive social change. Recycled Words n' Stuff (2016) a collection of short narratives, and essays of general interest.

30. FRAMEWORK FOR VIEWING CLASSROOM LEARNING

Individuals approach the teaching/learning process with relatively fixed attitudes. This predisposition was shaped by the early stages of knowledge base formation. Since learning about the unknown is directly related to the known, those students with weak foundations may turn into reluctant or obstinate learners and become indirectly influenced by peers more than the direct influence of the teacher. Managing their conduct normally will cause the teaching/learning process to be more difficult. Such students may need extra tutoring and personal attention. Family and community environment and mature attitudes about education influence this predisposition. Bonding with mature students and personality development are factors that assist in the formation of these learning attitudes.

CLASSIFICATION OF LEARNING ATTITUDES

Excellent Learners	Informal Learners	Reluctant Learners	Obstinate Learners
Have a strong desire to learn	Require a more relaxed, less structured process	Are cautious about partici-pating, but will follow the crowd	Are unwilling to change and difficult to manage

Normal healthy age-specific development together with positive influence from family and friends will produce an excellent student who desires to learn. Teaching such students is almost effortless because they are self-starters. The development of certain personality traits and individual characteristics may produce an informal learner who requires a more relaxed and less structured process, for learning. Such students may see things differently than others and develop study and work habits that may not fit the norm. In reality, these may not receive the highest grades in the class, but they may actually be the better learners with long-term benefits that predict personal and professional achievements. In some educational systems, the informal learner may be classified as a "C" student but will probably end up owning the business and hiring the excellent students to do the work. A list in history may verify this possibility. Some of the informal learners that ended up on top of the heap were Edison, Lincoln, Einstein, von Braun, Reagan, Kennedy, Clinton, Bush, and the list goes on and on.

Opportunity Equals Obligation -- Although many students are reluctant learners, all students have motives for their action. The task of the teacher is to understand these motives and provide an activity to assist the student toward their desired goals. Parents and family can assist, but the last-ditch stand is in the classroom. Teachers must be aware of what activates the motive of students to learn. Each opportunity is an obligation for the teacher. The classroom can change the world one student at a time. It is a privilege to be trusted as a teacher.

As a preschooler, Albert Einstein was sick in bed when his father gave him a compass. Einstein later recalled the excitement and wonder as he examined the mysterious powers of the compass. The needle seemed to move as if influenced by a distant force. There were no mechanical explanation for the moves and young Einstein perceived that some deep mystery was behind the movement of the compass hand. This curiosity led to Einstein's thinking about magnetic fields, gravity, inertia and light beams and gave him a life direction.

An uncle who was an engineer introduced young Albert to algebra calling it a "merry science." By age thirteen Einstein exhibited a predisposition for solving complicated problems in the field of applied mathematics. Writing an essay on theoretical physics at age 16, Einstein was well on his way to discovering the Theory of Relativity. The record shows that Einstein had difficulty with ordinary math and may not have received the necessary encouragement from teachers, but by age 40 Albert Einstein's life-applications would make him world famous. His journey toward greatness began as a sick preschooler studying the hands of a compass. This thoughtful gift from a sensitive parent and the later academic encouragement from an uncle produced an individual who changed the world. This also points to the joint influence of family members and teachers in intellectual achievements.

A human element behind today's satellite and space exploits, Werner von Braun, became interested in space as a small boy. This German-born scientist saw a drawing of a rocket streaking through space and sent for the booklet. The illustration caught the interest of young von Braun, but he was startled to find the booklet contained mostly sophisticated mathematical equations. Young von Braun disliked math and had difficulty with the subject in school, but this fact did not discourage this young scientist to be. His interest had been sparked, he had formalized a motive and a vehicle was discovered to facilitate his ultimate goal and his life-objective. He was interested in space, so some teacher unlocked the secrets and used his childhood memories to apply math solutions to his life-application. To learn more about space, he had to study math. With the encouragement of others, he made the choice, "If I must know math to learn about space then I will learn math." His motive to learn about space using the activity of improving math skills, even in spite of the struggles of War, he became the personification of man's struggle to rise above his environment and reach for higher goals. His life struggle and life applications still benefit the world.

The youthful dreams of many achieving individuals have provided a worthy life-direction. Abraham Lincoln's lofty ambitions were born as he counted the stars through the cracks in a cabin roof. Hard work and a difficult personal struggle for an adequate education developed basic gifts for debate and decision. With limited light from an open fireplace, Lincoln pressed the envelope of learning until he rose to the highest office in America and literally stabilized the future of the United States of America by confronting division, slavery, and injustice, and preserved a union that became a force for good in the world.

Thomas A. Edison describing his systematic and detailed life said, "I never did anything worth doing by accident." His intentionality produced hopes and dreams and materialized because he possessed and used untiringly a great inventive talent. In addition to perseverance, the real secret to Edison's achievements was that he saw all failure and disappointment as a learning experience and found a way to turn the negative aspects of his life and work into positive adventures.

All individuals desiring to be called "teacher" to be adequate to the task must learn this lesson and deal with negativity in a positive manner. This illustrates a basic rule in philosophy; one can never reach a positive conclusion beginning with a negative premise. A second construct of philosophy is appropriate here: a positive implies a negative. When a positive life-direction is determined there is confidence that much of the negativity of life can be avoided by applying the positive influence of parents and teachers.

Transformational Teachers -- A clear need for methodology suggests that a learning leader may be needed. When a process appears to be complicated, it may only be sophisticated and a teacher or instructor may direct the learner on a path through the maze. Once the footsteps are on the guided path, the process is no longer complicated and the learner can move forward with limited guidance. Teachers then become facilitators of learning.

Transformational teachers must conceptualize their roles significantly more than the classroom monitor, current learning leaders in the classroom, tutoring positions, and guidance counselors must become computer instructors, technology users and Internet surfers and not only talkers, chalkboard or whiteboard writers. Listening also advances the teaching/learning process. Teachers become facilitators in the process of self-directed learning. The tutors and classroom teachers operate as consultants; provide referrals and resources for the learner. The learning leader, regardless of the title, must establish an environment which encourages self-diagnosis, the formulation of objectives and the learner's ability for the design, implementation and continuation of learning strategies.

Twenty-first century learning leaders must be aware of the problems in a non-conventional educational environment and must be aware and utilize the available technology to enhance the learning experience. They need to be knowledgeable of the learner's physical, psychological, social, cultural and family environment and function in an appropriate manner to enhance an atmosphere conducive to self-directed learning. The teaching and learning philosophy and subsequent teaching style obviously form crucial elements in appropriate interface with self-directed learners. From a philosophical point of view, both pragmatism and existentialism seem least at odds with self-directed learning. The former has obvious advantages with its emphasis on experiential reality and the latter because of its basis on reality as existence (Gutek 1988).

In ancient sacred writings there was a follower of a Master Teacher who measured his life-purpose and achievements by articulating a controlling principle of his life, "This one thing I do...reaching forth for those things which are before." The positive reaching forward caused him to forget the negative things of the past. This was the focus of Saul of Tarsus on pleasing the Master Teacher and doing good for mankind that gave his life courage to overcome difficulties and confidence to face the future. He wrote to a young teacher, "And entrust the things you learned from me which were confirmed by many witnesses, to faithful men who will be competent to teach others also. (2 Timothy 2:2 EDNT) In the view of this teacher, the teaching profession was a perpetual assembly line turning out competent learners who were capable of becoming knowledgeable teachers.

Education and Life Applications -- Classroom leaders and the educational delivery system relate to modalities and mechanisms that include both necessity and possibility. Normally, teachers are qualified in educational philosophy, instructional and content delivery systems, basic human development, and under normal circumstance concentrate on the central task of education transacted and embodied in the teaching/learning process. All programs of education should have a singleness of purpose to complement and not compete with existing entities and institutions. Education should not attempt to do the work of faith-based entities or become preoccupied with sectarian thinking. Neither should education encroach on the purview of parents unless they are obviously dysfunctional or criminally neglectful. In such cases, remedial and surrogate discipline and guidance may be required to make the teaching/learning process work effectively. However, teachers and educational leaders should not rigidly adhere to a set of beliefs and fail to demonstrate tolerance for other points of view. All tax supported educational activities should be non-sectarian, non-profit, and non-discriminatory, but committed to the social and moral values of the community and society at large.

Teacher and Student Assessments -- Without a level playing field, the system cannot adequately evaluate teacher competence and student achievements. New teachers who are given a class of misfits or delinquents may appear or feel inadequate and become discouraged with the profession while experienced teachers are advanced to the "easy learners" and self-starters. The quality and capacity of classroom instructions also impacts student learning. Because of many dysfunctional families, classroom teachers are often expected to compensate for parental and/or community failures. This is a burden that becomes a bridge too far for many teachers.

Classroom teachers should not be expected to do the work of parents or community authorities when their task is basic education. That task is to stimulate interest in the subject matter, arouse a spirit of inquiry, and get the student involved in the learning process. When teachers are forced to become disciplinarians or truant officers, to create an atmosphere conducive to learning, the teaching/learning process is hindered. Unacceptable classroom behavior distracts from classroom objectives and imposes deficiencies on the whole class. Teachers are weak substitutes for loving parents and the school classroom an atmosphere totally different from what exists in the local community. There is no magic in the classroom that easily corrects home and community failures. In fact, parents and family are considered more important to academic achievement than are budgets, curriculum, teachers, textbooks or classroom equipment. However, where the family and previous instruction models have failed the student, educators must practice tough love and positive remedial education and seek to constructively and creatively solve the learning distractions of students. This must also include the general protection and welfare of the teaching staff and school property. All programs of education must encourage mutually beneficial relationships with parents, organizations, and communities which share the same basic moral values.

As a state or community sponsored program, the school system should provide directions for academic development and problem solving skills that are geared to the transitions demanded of students moving from a parent-based to a teacher-based learning model and then to a self-study process. This does not mean that parents are not involved in their children's education; it simply means that qualified teachers are guiding the process of a standardized educational program and seeking positive parental assistance. It means that parents must never neglect their children's education and must express concern and provide assistance regardless of the age-specific level of education involved. It also suggests that there will come a time when the student outgrows the need for classroom support and may become more dependent on guidance from the family before they can become an independent learner using all past learning to gain needed knowledge useful for a career or profession. However, students never outgrow their need for family or for academic guidance and encouragement. Without such direction and support that inspires confidence, the real world can become an intimidating place.

Regardless of classroom activities, learning is self-paced and should be flexible and structured to achieve optimum benefit from academic interface, independent study, parental assistance, faculty guidance and peer support. All students work from a personal knowledge base and experience to utilize classroom or subject content and enhance competence and performance. The teaching/ learning interface should be structured to precipitate transformational change through aggressive learning and innovative instruction. The objective is to gain new knowledge which may be used to answer questions and used in present and future problem solving.

By analyzing the structure of the educational environment and society in general from the perspective of moral and ethical needs, a group of transformational learning leaders can make a difference in advancing beneficial changes in the objectives and practices of education. Such an educational program requires an evident balance between what educators believe and what students actually do. Thus, the curriculum and instruction must be related to the background of the student and appropriate to the community. It must be evenhanded, unprejudiced by present community problems, and adequately balanced with commitments to the past deposit of moral truth upon which ethical and moral behavior is based.

This commitment requires recognition of what constitutes past moral and ethical behavior, but in no way relieves supervisors and instructors of responsibility to understand present society and to seek solutions for current problems and learning difficulties. The system must clearly synthesize moral and ethical foundations of community into a philosophy of productive social change and service to society. The educational process should culminate in both an ethical and productive citizen who supports the common values of society. This is transformational education. Systematic teaching is a general term for a pedagogic-structured style of teaching which are preplanned to produce specific learning outcomes.

In the present age of technology and 24/7/365 exposure to global issues, to accomplish the transformational changes required to advance the teaching/learning process, the educational system must move beyond pedagogic methods to more advanced andragogic and synergetic learning designs. Andragogy is teaching students as mature learners regardless of age. It also includes the concept that education is not only vocational but general preparation for life and lifelong learning. Andragogy fosters the concept that education is a process that continues throughout life and is not limited to a classroom, age, or the presence of a teacher. The concept of synergy is learning from one another and has impact on all aspects of peer interaction in education. Synergetic designs are a systematic approach to learning in which the members of small groups learn from one another through structured interactions; thus, the idea of synergy in learning. Challenge and stimulation are created through social situations where real and felt needs may be satisfied. All education must provide learning activities and materials from which knowledge or insights can be acquired and create designs—instructions for both individual and group action—that can stimulate learning. (Mouton 1984)

Conflict and Creativity -- Transformational instruction must go beyond pedagogic methods to include the construct of Synectics, a term used in writing on creativity. Greek in origin, the word means the bringing together of separated and seemingly irrelevant ideas or information. It is a systematic attempt to search all aspects of a problem creatively. In reality it is the development of the creative capacity of a student. Brainstorming is one techniques used in this process. Synectics also involves using mechanisms that make the strange familiar and the familiar strange to extend the creative imagination. Traditional pedagogic methods should be used only in the early stages of education or when necessary to instruct, tutor or communicate new content and when a specialized competency is required to move forward.

The characters that make the Chinese word "conflict" include crisis and opportunity. The English word is less revealing but has some of the same concepts when one considers the synonyms; such as, contention, contest, struggle, etc. In other words conflict may lead one to become creative. Creativity and invention are required when the way forward is blocked or unseen. When an individual is able to handle conflict or two opposing concepts and somehow merge them into one new construct they are being creative. Some businesses are able to both sell a product and nurture customers, others combine competition with discipline and create opportunities that advance their market share, the founding fathers of the United States of America were able to combine freedom and accountability and establish an enduring and responsible nation. This idea has explosive meaning for education and the teaching/learning process.

The classroom model stands in opposition to the distance education mechanisms, and the pedagogic processes are counter-productive when over used with the more innovative models related to Andragogy and synergetic learning designs. When the emphasis on content overpowers process both teaching and learning are hindered. However, when an experienced teacher clearly understands the predisposition and maturity of learners, they can effectively combine pedagogy and the more interactive designs and greatly facilitate the learning process. When a teacher understands that the goal of teaching is to make the learner self-sufficient, the conflict is resolved and learning opportunities bust forth much as the morning sunrise does after a dark and stormy night.

The pioneer leaders of nations and the men and women of past generations invented, developed, manufactured, built, constructed, fought great wars, won significant victories, and achieved great things without the technological and scientific support available today. In a day when high school drop-outs can become National Network News Anchors, when men with "C" averages in education can be elected to the highest positions in the land, and when individuals leave college because they are bored with the process but create major corporations, it is time to rethink education and do everything possible to improve the teaching/learning process. Part of that improvement is to develop self-actualizing, self-paced, self-confident, and self-sufficient learners.

Assumptions about Serious Study -- To learn from a written text, one must see the author of the text as a real person, a learning leader, and the text as an objective body of knowledge and utilize a methodical approach to comprehend the content. The information, facts, and data included in an objective text are distinct form the reader's interpretation. Consequently, the reader must be objective in viewing the written material. There is no absolute objectivity or pure induction; therefore, a systematic method is required to interpret written material. A student must view a written work from the author's perspective to arrive at a sound understanding. Subjectivity in analysis corrupts the intended meaning of the content. The author of a text must be considered a personal instructor with concern and interest in the reader. The author has many of the same qualities and concerns as does the classroom teacher.

Constructive change in education requires dynamic structures and mechanisms appropriate for the twenty-first century. Using transformational concepts, leaders can map a path to positive social change in the teaching/learning process and create a curriculum and instructional components that will open new thinking and learning patterns in the classroom and beyond.

31. HOPE FOR A VIABLE CHRISTIANITY

The only hope for a viable Christianity in America is an internal redirection of the soul that brings with it a personal commitment to the cardinal tenets of the Christian Faith and a spirit of cooperation and trust. In addition to the problems of "name brand Christianity" and "freeze framed theology", One Lord, One Faith and One Baptism has become 300 denominations with antagonistic leaders, competing agendas, and opposing methodologies. Leaders must take the initiative to bring renewal and restoration to the congregation and make evangelism and missions central to the local programming.

Is the progressive decline of Christianity in America inevitable? Is the character and social fabric of a pluralistic society so complicated that Christianity cannot work in American? Evidence exists that Christianity could work if small changes could be made in both the attitude and the action of professing Christians. In isolated areas individual Christians are practicing their faith effectively and some local congregations are alive and growing. Sadly, this is not true of the total Christian movement in America.

For the most part, congregations in America seem to be fragmented, stagnant, and unable to communicate a unified message to the public.

Why does Christianity fail in America? What is the inferior operation that weakens the witness? The Christian message ceases to be a viable expression of faith when congregations:

- fail to accentuate commonalties
- fail to associate with local culture
- fail to embrace personal behavior
- fail to develop quality
- fail to build people
- fail to produce a melting pot
- fail to develop Christian culture
- fail to reproduce relational theology
- fail to stand on principle
- fail to promote heritage
- fail to espouse substance
- fail to augment the value of families

The blueprint for constructing an effective local congregation would be to take a positive stand and strive to move forward in all the areas where the congregation now fails to measure up to Great Commission. Until the areas of difficulty are understood, a superior congregation will not develop. The diagnosed failures must be corrected before a plan of action can be executed.

In 1967 Clyde Reid, in his work on preaching, declared the American pulpit to be empty:

The pulpit today is empty in the sense that there is often no message heard, no results seen, and no power felt. The emptiness of which I speak is an absence of meaning, a lack of relevance, and a failure in communication. To be sure, this is a relative emptiness, not absolute. But it is emptiness, nevertheless. In the intervening decades the empty pulpit syndrome has produced a half-filled church with half-hearted commitment to the basic tenets of the Christian Faith.

In the intervening decades the empty pulpit syndrome has produced a half-filled church with half-hearted commitment to the basic tenets of the Christian Faith. Any defense of the viability of Christianity in America today is to suggest that the structures of the past are good enough for today and the future. This is certainly not true in any other aspect of life or history. The church is made up of people and people change. The church exists in a society, and societies change. Change is the one constant factor of modern life. The structure, message and communication of American Christianity must change to maintain any semblance of viability in the future.

As America enters the Twenty-first Century the situation is even worse. Congregations have been unable to bridge the great fixed gulf between Church and State or to reduce the negative effect of an intrusive government into the life-style of church members. Although American Presidents have been identified with Christianity and related to a specific denomination, the "pulpit" of the Presidency together with the combined pulpits of thousands of churches were unable to stem the tide of moral decay and progressive debauchery in American life. Clergy involvement in public life and political causes have not prevented discrimination or eliminated injustice in America.

Drastic change is required to prepare American Christianity for the "communications super-highway" and the certain cultural and technological changes coming with the Twenty-first Century. In America, a cultural framework for doctrine has created a brand name concept for Protestant congregations. This development was based on the writings of past theologians and produced a freeze frame theology not relevant to the present generation.

Many congregations have failed to transmit adequate experiential knowledge of the Christian life to succeeding generations to make genuine converts. This, coupled with the mobility of society, has produced complex and confusing relationships within American congregations. Consequently, many unintentionally hinder the conversion of the next generation to the Christian Faith. To make Christianity viable in the Twenty-first Century, there must be an internal redirection of the soul that includes a return to a personal Christian experience, accountability and commitment.

32. WHO WILL FIGHT THE AMALEKITES?

The Amalekites were an ancient and nomadic marauding people who usually sided with the enemies of God's People. Moses felt the wrath of an unprovoked attack on the Israelites for which God decreed continual war and ultimate obliteration. (Exodus 17:8ff) Amalek in an ambush attached the "hindmost" of the Israelite troop coming out of Egypt, "even all that were feeble behind you, when you were faint and weary; and he feared not God." Israel was told to blot out the remembrance of Amalek from under heaven, and God warned "thou shalt not forget it." Joshua and the spies encountered the Amalekites in Canaan where the Amalekites together with the Canaanites overcame Israel. (Deuteronomy 25:18, 19).

During the period of the Judges, the Amalekites sided with the Ammonites and Moabites against the Israelites and with the Midanites against Gideon. Saul was told to utterly destroy the Amalekites for their animosity and ambush against the Israelites, but failed in this important mission and after Saul's sons were killed in battle and Saul attempted to take his own life failed; it was an Amalekite who came and finished the task and took Saul's crown to David. It was King David who later subdued the Amalekites. (2 Samuel 1:1f)

Lay Aside Every Weight and Sin -- One must lay aside every weight and sin that so easily overwhelm. Addictions that control must be conquered. Bad habits that destroy your testimony must be broken. Vocabulary that does not honor God must be replaced. Protect the health of your body and mind. These are the little "Amalekites" that ambush you and take advantage of your weaknesses. Believers must always be on the alert and ready to defend themselves and others from evil forces. Remember the old adage: "An ounce of prevention is worth a pound of cure!" Destroying the "Amalekites" in your life is necessary for full obedience and a testimony worthy of the price of redemption.

Avoidance is easier than recuperation and recovery. Another old adage speaks loudly to this issue: "A bird with a broken wing never flies as high!" If cleanliness is next to godliness, then prevention is akin to holiness. To separate from evil, to remain free from the normal sins of the human race, and to build a life of Christian living requires the assistance of the Holy Spirit and complete obedience to the Captain of our Salvation: Jesus Christ. The things that hinder your spiritual progress are "little Amalekites" and are bold against all good because they fear not God. Cromwell, an early English churchman, had a motto written on his pocket Bible in Latin—*qui cessat esse melior cessat esse bonus*—"he who ceases to be better ceases to be good." Bad habits are easy to pick up, but difficult to put down. In fact, it takes about 21 days to break a bad habit by substituting another activity or behavior; but only one slip and the habit is back stronger than before. Remember the scripture about the devil returning and finding the house cleaned; seven more devils moved into the house. The latter end was worse that the beginning. (Luke 11:24-26) Care must be taken when dealing with the "bad stuff" the little Amalekites; assistance and guidance are needed. Vigilance is required. Perseverance is necessary. Spiritual boldness is helpful. Putting on the whole armor of the Spirit is the best shield against the return of the "things" that pull you down.

An Effort to Rally the Troops -- A philosophical dichotomy has developed between how a person sees himself/herself and how a person behaves. The eyes of ethical leaders have become accustomed to the moral darkness and their minds blinded to the light of truth. Without moral leadership, the public has grown soft on sin, accepting personal sins, even in public places, as an unalienable right. These "cherished sins" speak loudly to the youth: "What I do does not affect who I am!" This construct is certainly not verifiable by Holy Scripture. Although a few aspects of systematic theology may be misconstrued to suggest that one may live anyway he/she pleases them just because once upon a time they accepted Christ's forgiveness. This is far from orthodox teaching and is a dangerous idea.

General Good Suffers -- The general good suffers when one is not accountable for private behavior. Jesus called this the "leaven of the Pharisees." Sin cannot long be hidden. Breaking God's commandments is rebellion and grieves the Spirit of God. (Ephesians 4:30) Scripture declared that secret sins would be made public and that gossip whispered in the closet would be shouted from the housetop. With hidden sin to be ultimately uncovered, why does anyone persist in a life of immorality? What you fail to destroy may well destroy you!

Victory is Lost -- Spiritual victory is normally lost because of a fear of confrontation. Is the spirit of the Biblical Prophet dead and buried? Is there no one to say to the King, "Thou art the man?" Not only do evil forces assault individual Christians, there seems to be an all-out warfare against Christian ethics and faith-based morality, or anything that hints at the essential elements of a Christian Heritage. Is nothing sacred? What is next: "In God we trust" on the coins or "Under God" in the Pledge of Allegiance? All who would live the Christian life or become leaders for the Christian cause must resist evil forces or ultimate victory is surely lost. When one stumbles and brings disgrace to the Christian cause, all believers suffer the stigma of insincerity. Again, where is the spirit of the Biblical Prophet that declares there is sin in the camp?

Disgrace through Immorality -- As one good leader after another falls in disgrace through immorality, it is time to declare war on the forces of Satan and stand in the gap and pray.   Leaders must have clean and upright living to validate the message of God's saving grace. People will not drink from a contaminated well. They will not listen to a false prophet in the ministry for the money. The people will not long follow a political leader who does not demonstrate a moral and ethical foundation. The Christian life must be lived in power and glory for the world to see the value of walking with God.

A Strategic Resistance -- Believers must live the resurrected life and walk in the Spirit to demonstrate that Satan has no power over us or the work that God has called us to do.   Believers must organize a strategic resistance to all things evil. The Church must make a new and fresh commitment to right living, in order to protect the witness of the saints and the message of the gospel. Believers must join the over comers and enlist in the battle to behave what they believe. Moral leaders must rally the troops at a personal level and develop a strategy of resistance; however, the most potent weapons are personal prayer and the guidance of the Holy Spirit. The church must stand ready to act responsibly. Believers must work together as saints triumphant!

Gilboa -- a Place of Defeat and Victory -- Gilboa, a significant place in Israel's military history, where the Lord instructed Gideon to reduce his forces so that it would be obvious that God was responsible for the victory against the Midianites and Amalekites. Gideon obeyed the Lord and Gideon's tiny band of 300 routed the enemy (Judges 7:1-25) and God received the credit. Gideon's obedience brought victory in one of the most remarkable conflicts of Israel's history.

It was also at Gilboa that Saul's disobedience in failing to utterly destroy the Amalekites was finally punished. After the battle was lost and Saul attempted suicide, an Amalekite came on the scene. Saul asked him to finish the botched job of suicide so he would not fall into the hands of the enemy alive. It was an Amalekite that stood upon Saul's dying body and made the final strike that finished Saul. It was an Amalekite that took Saul's crown. Saul's disobedience of not utterly destroying all the Amalekites returned to finish Saul. The things he failed to destroy in the end destroyed him. This should be a lesson to all. (2 Samuel 1:1f)

33. DISCIPLESHIP

Modern man has changed the term "Christian" to meet lower personal standards of various sectarian groups. In many circles, the term no longer means a true believer in Jesus Christ: one who has forsaken all, denied self, taken up the Cross, and is daily following Jesus Christ. One must return to the original term which described the early followers of Christ to properly define the Christian experience. This book brings the terms "disciple" and "Christian" together because it is believed that an understanding of Christian discipleship will give a proper perspective to the whole of Christian living.

A declaration that Jesus Christ has all power prefaced the Great Commission, and it was climaxed by the promise that Christ would always be with His people. The strength of the early church came when they discovered that life is a cooperative venture with God. This changed the disciples into Christ-like men, who became a powerful force for truth in the world. With one voice they proclaimed

Christ's death, burial, and resurrection; in "one accord" they witnessed to His living presence. All divisions vanished, and they went forth to bear witness in the power of unity. With this clearly in mind, believers, today, must go forth living the word in every aspect of life. Then it is easy to sacrifice; then it is easy to serve; then it is easy to live and to walk the way of Christian discipleship, because discipleship is a vital aspect of Christian living.

This work was originally written in 1962 as a Church Training Course for workers in Christian Education. It is presented again because of the need for Discipleship remains. Only a few changes from the original text were made for this edition to make it more gender neutral. The reader is reminded that the "masculine gender bias" that existed in the 1962 edition could not be readily changed. Times have changed and readers expect things to be gender neutral; however, the Bible has not changed and the quotations are from the KJV that remains somewhat masculine.

The present task of the author is to write new books, but a few out of print books are being sold on the web at high prices. This reissued edition is to keep the content in the existent literature and bring the material at a reasonable price to new readers. After all, the basic concept of scriptural-based discipleship has not changed, but there are fewer active Christian disciples in the local churches of the 21st Century. Perhaps this scriptural-based text will shed new light on the old message of Christian discipleship.

34. TYPES OF INQUIRY

Despite all of modern science's perceived wizardry and high-powered technology, human beings can inquire in only two basic ways, analysis, and synthesis. In analysis, they separate a perceived whole into its parts; in synthesis, they combine perceived parts into wholes. By these two actions, humans investigate existence. All observation is built on these two types of inquiry. Likewise, thought systems are dichotomous, being fundamentally inductive or deductive. Inquiry systems and thought systems are not unrelated. Inquiry can be made in both scientific and nonscientific disciplines through analysis and synthesis using deductive and inductive logic.

Two methods of correct thinking (reasoning) derive from this basic dichotomy of human inquiry --deduction and induction. Deductive logic moves from the perceived whole (the general case) to a part (the specific case). Inductive logic moves from the perceived parts (specific cases) to the whole (the general case). When inductive or deductive logic chains are performed unconsciously in the human brain, the resulting transformation is termed a hunch or and intuition.

Both synthesis and analysis, with their corresponding logic's, induction, and deduction, are used generally. Science involves human experience and knowledge remembers or stores experience. Consequently, the controlled experiment is a means of formally, rigorously, and objectively experiencing and recording a well-defined human event.

This deductive process involving analysis is what commonly comes to mind when one thinks of scientific

process. While few would deny that scientific analysis
has made possible the technological breakthroughs of the
modern age, many neglect the contribution of synthesis and
the process of induction to these rapid and far-reaching
advances. Synthesis is generally the process of establishing
the assumptions from which interpretations are deduced.
Interpretations deduced from false assumptions about the
human experience cannot be empirically supported.

Graduate-level reading is sophisticated research. It
is a search for something in particular rather than reading
for general information. Developmental readings are
much the same as looking for a word in a dictionary or
looking up a subject in an encyclopedia. One does not read
the entire work. The effort is to search for something in
particular. When the rules are followed it is not a difficult
process. For example, looking for material on Zoology in an
encyclopedia, one does not begin reading in the "A" section.
The process of selecting information for a written document
is simplified with logic and common sense.

The etymological meaning of the word research is
"seek again." Today this word is commonly used to describe
a wide range of activities concerned with human inquiry.
Literally, the derived meaning suggests two fundamental
characteristics, (1) diligence of inquiry and (2) a temporal
relationship only to the present and past, although a basic
purpose may be to extract a meaning that can be applied to
the future.

Perhaps it is this latter characteristic that fixed the
earliest inquiries on questions of origin and existence. A
diligent searching again of the past reveals that existence,
moving over time, has order, patterns, and sequences. The
discovery of relationships that persisted overtime made

it possible to seek answers to questions about the future. Predictive instruments, such as calendars, were based on observed recurring patterns of the past. In reading one learns through the same process.

As humans wrote down their observations, the effort to understand what was written began. To understand and interpret different aspects of human existence, various groups of scholars began to devise different schemes, but all used the basic method of inquiry. Eventually, sets of such methods were accepted as reliable by consensus of particular groups. Different groups were concerned with different aspects of human inquiry; and, consequently, the methodologies that evolved differed from group to group.

In its early history, research served at least a two-fold objective: It sharpened the intellectual concerns of humans, and it assisted in developing theories to explain the universe. Human enlightenment was its goal. The earliest questions related to the universe, the grand scheme, not to such parts as the economic, social, cultural, political and anthropological aspects of human existence. Gradually, scientific prediction methods were adapted to more and more specific questions. As adaptation proliferated, disciplines emerged within the general process of scientific research.

Early in its development, the lack of systematic and objective observation restricted the progress of research. Thinking itself was not necessarily systematic. Overcoming this restriction required developing a way to systematically think about thinking. Thus, logic emerged.

Attributed to the Greeks, the early development of logic took the form of deductive reasoning. This system of logic derives conclusions from generalizations, that is, universally accepted assumptions. The idea that "the whole" influences "the part" is a principle of deductive thought. The philosophy of Socrates and Plato gave direction to the developments of thought and produced early concepts of social relationships among humans.

Aristotle continued this reshaping of human imagination by analyzing ideas based on generalizations that were inductively obtained. He observed commonalties among many objects and processes and concluded that these common traits probably existed for all such objects and processes. His relentless quest for new assertions and "facts" based on field observations added the dimension of empiricism to scientific research. When such concepts conflicted with pristine religious authority, they were often rejected by the community. Curiosity persisted, however, and people with academic orientation began to rely on "facts" that could be empirically confirmed. Notwithstanding the progress in human inquiry, the fall of Greek and Roman civilization caused dogma to be re-emphasized and empirical investigations to be largely neglected.

The Renaissance Period revived the thought process that encouraged a search for new knowledge. Major discoveries, such as new continents, expanded thinking about physics, economics, society, and human behavior generally. The age of Galileo and Newton strengthened the intellectual process of scientific inquiry.

Numerous thinkers followed (e. g., Sir Thomas More, Machiavelli, Bacon, Hobbes, and Locke), each offering various insights into the nature and the function of the human experience. All, in one manner or another sought to distinguish reality from fiction and superstition. Gradually, the reality that concerned scientific investigation came to be viewed in terms of physical attributes that could be empirically confirmed. The Industrial Revolution witnessed a great emergence of intellectuals who continued inquiry into diverse social phenomena and added technological inventions. These thinkers developed increasingly more rigorous methods of research. As a consequence, philosophical and mathematical advances produced a dramatic increase in the number and variety of scientific discoveries. These could not be ignored and had major impact on human thought.

So rooted in the earliest awareness of a need for knowledge and the continuing search by generations of thinkers, the systematic process of investigation emerge, in spite of the hurdles of vested interests and lack of support from the general populous. The present concept of scientific methodology began to form during medieval times and developed into a full body of concepts and constructs in the modern age.

A basic problem in understanding an author's words relates to the language and culture. When words or thoughts are translated from one language and a particular culture to another the meaning changes. These changes often go unnoticed and individuals apply a current definition to the words. In fact the meaning of words is in people. Words in English may not mean the same as when they were written. A few examples from Holy Scripture may validate this point.

A classic misunderstanding of the Great Commission has produced a self-defeating theology of coercion in an effort to compel people to "go and do" when the intent of the commission was clearly "as you go make disciples."

An aorist participle was translated as an imperative that made an indirect command "As you go make disciples" into a direct command "Go!" The intent of the participle was personal action as individuals traveled about their daily lives. The present life-style evangelism is the closest to a clear understanding of what Christ meant in the commission. The Christian way was to be a life-style and the making of disciples an automatic part of the process. (Matthew 28:19, 20 EDNT)

Another translation difficulty is found in Titus 2:14 the translation of "peculiar." In 1611 the word had the meaning of private property or that which belongs to a person to the exclusion of others. The KJV translators took the Latin *peculium* from Roman law meaning the property which a son, wife, or slave might hold as his own, or to be over and above. This was clearly understood in Medieval England because the King and Lords had total claim on their subjects. Although it may be good theology: that Jesus died to make believers His personal possession. The word "peculiar" was misunderstood by the early Holiness Movement in the US which established a peculiar dress and life-style to be different from the rest of the world. One can easily see how the word "peculiar" meant one thing in early England and another in parts of America.

Another word that creates problems in contemporary America is the word "blessed." In the Old Testament days and in early England the word "bless" meant "blood or blood-related." The legal construct of inheritance in ancient times was established so property could be passed to blood relatives. Also in the Old Testament the first born received a double portion of the inheritance because of birth order and blood-related priority.

35. COMPLICATED VS. SOPHISTICATED

Research is not complicated; it is sophisticated. Social scientific research is an invention of humans and has been developed over time. This refinement causes complexity and specialized knowledge to be required to simplify the methods and the process. Once those methods and procedures are understood the methodology no longer appears to be complicated.

A Logical Dichotomy -- A logical dichotomy in the research process is clear: first, the process of developing a plan or proposal, and second, the gathering and analysis of data and preparing the conclusions and implications. The proposal is a "we – process." The academic institution has regulations and procedures which must be followed. A comprehensive review of relevant literature is necessary to place the research problem in the context of the thinking of others. The proposal process is also guided by institutional mentors and advisors. This makes the research proposal a "we project." Notwithstanding, the "we-ness" of the proposal process, the academic research process, that of gathering and analyzing data, testing hypotheses, and reporting findings is a most "personal process." The actual research is a "me" thing!

TWO PHILOSOPHIC RAZORS
(principles or witty sayings)

Ockham's Razor -- is a principle attributed to the 14th-century English logician and Franciscan friar, William of Ockham. The principle stated that the explanation of any phenomenon should make as few assumptions as possible, eliminating those that make no difference in the observable predictions of the explanatory hypothesis or theory. The principle is often expressed in Latin as the *lex parsimoniae* ("law of <u>parsimony</u>" or "law of succinctness"): *"entia non sunt multiplicanda praeter necessitatem",* roughly translated as "entities must not be multiplied beyond necessity."

This is often paraphrased as ***All other things being equal, the simplest solution is the best.*** In other words, when multiple competing theories are equal in other respects, the principle recommends selecting the theory that introduces the fewest assumptions and postulates the fewest entities. It is more often taken today as a <u>heuristic</u> <u>maxim</u> (rule of thumb) that advises economy, parsimony, or simplicity, especially in the scientific speculation. In this sense, Ockham's Razor becomes useful in the area of social research.

Hanlon's Razor – is a corollary philosophic principle called Hanlon's Razor is similar to Ockham's Razor and was simply stated, ***Do not attribute to malice what can be explained by stupidity.*** A similar witty saying has been attributed to William James. Witty sayings have little place in social research, but it is always good to keep Hanlon's razor in mind.

A most reasonable approach to social research is to learn the basic steps *and develop memory of the process. In* this way, the research becomes automatic and comfortable process. When one learns the basic keys, they enter a comfort zone and the process is no longer complicated.

36. A SPECIFIC NEED

The work on social scientific research is an effort to meet a specific need. The social professions are confronted with an increasing volume of relevant "scientific" information. Since they are one step closer to the ultimate application of basic knowledge -- life applications -- than applied sciences, professions constitute a final mixing bowl of disciplinal knowledge. The information they use to construct their purpose-directed thought systems is often the product of both pure and applied science, as well as physical, biological, and social. In the past, the training of professionals has not given adequate attention to the questions of what constitutes scientific information and how scientific research relates to the professions.

This is an effort to provide introductory answers to these questions in a manner that facilitates intermediate and advanced investigations by its readers. It may be used before or after the study of mathematics and statistics. Mathematical notation is minimized and any notation used should be explained in the text. The text incorporates a systems view of existence. This view makes it possible to efficiently integrate diverse disciplines of thought. James Grier Miller's living systems theory is used to provide the reader with a comprehensive conceptual framework by which knowledge accumulated in the various scientific disciplines may be interrelated and studied.

Science is concerned with consistent thinking and observation. Consistent systems of thought have been developed that make it possible for two independent persons who are provided with the same premises to arrive at the same conclusions. Likewise, methods of observation have been devised to insure that independent observers can record a particular observation in a manner that recognizes it as the same observation. Such public thought and observations processes are fundamental to all scientific investigation. We explain how measurement theory provides a basis for consistent quantitative thought systems that describe observations.

Complexity is a major obstacle to scientific investigation. Consequently, simplification methods must be employed. Modern scientific research widely uses statistical inference to overcome the complexity of measuring all objects of interest. Generally, statistical inference is based on a combination of measurement theory and involves procedures of hypothesis testing. It is important to know how these three important elements of scientific research are related and, in fact, integrated.

Finally, all social researchers must understand how hypothesis testing is achieved within the confines of controlled observation by proper research design. It is important to realize that all "scientific studies" are not necessarily good science. Common research designs must be understood in terms of control that are sacrificed as one moves from true experimentation to quasi- experimentation or to weak partial research designs.

Researchers need both an introduction handbook and a detailed guide extensive scientific research. This dual objective may be accomplished by succinctly over-viewing important building blocks of scientific research and providing additional references for in-depth study of issues, theory, procedures, and methods. The best use of basic textbooks is to first study them in the context of a philosophy of research course, followed by intermittent references as one progresses through an in-depth study of scientific research. For those in a formal research degree program, the initial study social scientific research should be early in the program and then be used to keep the "big picture" in focus as the candidate progress in their thesis/ dissertation projects.

Additional uses for books on basic social research include a desk reference for seasoned researchers to focus on specific investigations, a supplementary text for introductory statistics and research design courses, and a primary text for a much needed, but rarely provided, philosophy of social scientific research course for all involved in research related to positive social change.

37. A BLIND MAN AND AN ELEPHANT

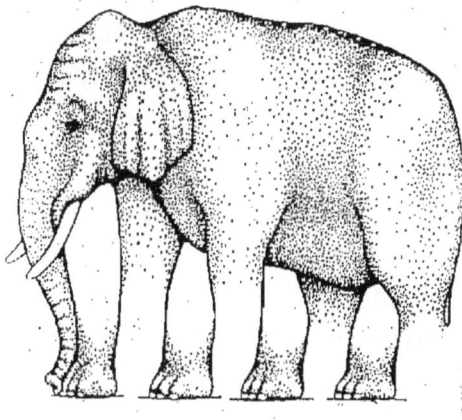

Social research is similar to a man blind from birth attempting to describe an elephant he has never seen. Based on prior knowledge of other animals and the human anatomy, he would attempt to identify and count elements he understood; such as, appendages, eyes, ears, etc. When the description was completed, the elephant would look much like a horse designed by a committee: a camel. A great deal may be learned in the process, but the picture would still be incomplete. This is true of the research process. One learns many things, but in the end much is left unknown. Those items remaining unknown become the subject for the next research project.

Qualitative and Quantitative Aspects of Research Qualitative and quantitative research are both necessary to accomplish social scientific research. Qualitative research is necessary to uncover the problem and analyze previous research on the subject and quantitative research is necessary to test the assumptions and hypotheses formulated on the subject. The two methods of research support one another and are not in opposition, nor is one considered more scholarly than the other. The precise nature of the research problem or question determines whether research will be predominantly qualitative or quantitative in terms of the research methodology. Each method requires a distinct approach to the solution of the problem.

The nature of the research design will determine whether the emphasis or weight of the dissertation falls on one side or the other of the quantitative -- qualitative dichotomy. Quantitative research is concerned primarily with measuring or assigning numbers to variables in a research hypothesis to determine the quantitative significance. Qualitative research is meant to signify that the research problem or question is being studied with reference to its historicity, essential ideas, or unique characteristics. Students should understand the nature and importance of each method and how both fit into the research process. A decision as to which method to stress should not be made until the candidate develops a full research proposal.

Qualitative research requires exhaustive logic and literature documentation to support each aspect of the research. In quantitative research the Literature Reviews is comprehensive, but not exhaustive. The literature places the problem in the context of current research and normally becomes a vital part of the proposal and final research report. It is a comprehensive review of published material related to the hypotheses proposed for the research and a current awareness search in journals for the past three years. A rigid design and statistical process supports the research conclusions.

In qualitative research, an exhaustive literature review must deal with the whole subject area as background support for the problem in the present study. For example, a qualitative study on a religious denomination dealing with a particular social or doctrinal issue would require an exhaustive review of the history of the denomination as it related to the problem at hand. Those who do qualitative dissertations normally have writing and publication experience, bachelors and master's degrees in the subject field, and/or extensive doctoral courses in the content area. One cannot jump into a qualitative study without an exhaustive effort to place the problem in the historical context of the environment under study. Finding the sources is often the greatest difficulty.

One major concern in the qualitative area deals with the conclusions. How does one support the conclusions and exclude rival explanations? This requires exhaustive work. Seminaries, some departments in universities, and some doctorates of lesser quality than the PhD, permit qualitative research, but universities that offer the PhD-type degree prefer scientific research that includes statistical support. The better universities that accept qualitative dissertations normally require logic chains and Boolean logic in support of conclusions. The Boolean approach is a mathematical system originally devised for the analysis of symbolic logic, in which all variables have the value of either zero or one. It is this process that is used to support the digital computer system. The use of statistics to test a hypothesis is much simpler than the extensive use of Boolean logic.

Research supported by quantitative means is normally much shorter than qualitative research. Supporting conclusions by logic and Boolean algebra requires critical thinking, sound reasoning, and good journalistic skills. A few statistics can save many written pages and provide almost instant support for the conclusions made in a quantitative study. For example, qualitative research needs a preponderance of the evidence (perhaps 95%) to support personally reasoned conclusions. While quantitative research can reject a null hypotheses at the statistical .05 level of confidence and consequently support the original research hypotheses. By going in the back door and finding a small relationship or difference, the null hypothesis may be rejected; this automatically supports or confirms the original assumption or hypothesis. This could mean the difference in 25 pages versus 5 pages of support for one hypotheses or conclusion.

Qualitative research is historical and theoretical in nature and indicates a study of primary and secondary sources that recount the past history and narrates the present context of the research topic. Theoretical research is a study of sources in order to discover, explain, formulate, compare, or analyze theories or ideas associated with the research topic. In historical and theoretical research, it is crucial to have authentic and accurate research data. This data comes through primary and secondary sources.

The sources are used to determine the value and accuracy of any research assumption or conclusion. The veracity of these sources comes through external and internal criticism. External criticism determines the authenticity of the sources. Internal criticism evaluates their accuracy or worth of the data. Once the credibility of the primary and secondary sources is established, the researcher critiques these sources in relation to the particular problem or question under study. Both historical and theoretical research is to be as exhaustive as possible.

One of the reasons faculty directs students to social scientific research rather than historical studies, is the content and academic background is not normally there to take the qualitative approach. It is not that qualitative research is substandard; it is mainly that statistically supported research is usually easier for the inexperienced researcher. Doctoral candidates are normally writing a dissertation as a first effort at a major project. One wants conclusions to be accepted and statistical support for conclusions are normally more readily accepted by both academia and the organizations and institutions related to the research problem. Often, without exhaustive documentation in support of conclusions, the reasoning or logic can be easily questioned. Academics are not opposed to this kind of study, but the methodology is difficult to teach because it is learned through trial and error and experience. Also, the length of time is exhausting and the final data less appreciated. When students make mistakes in reasoning and logic in a short research papers, one can imagine what could happen in a long qualitative research project.   In my judgment, statistics is much easier to learn than Boolean algebra and/or logic. The thought is enough to make one want to learn statistics.

38. A WORKABLE MARRIAGE

Conversation is the key to a workable marriage. There must be dialogue, mutual exchange, general discussions, small talk, quick chats, and long term one-to-one, heart-to-heart exchange. Only this process can bring about true respect and love in an extended relationship.

How It All Began!

Seeing a young lady in church without a man for several weeks, I became interested. Observing her devotion, her interest in music, her involvement with children, and her general demeanor, my heart spoke to me. I think it was my heart, maybe it was my mind, or even my aloneness. Regardless, when one gets a message from the inner self, it has a compelling voice, and demands action.

The church where I saw her was near Dobbins Air Force Base in Georgia. I never saw a man with her, so I began to ponder. Being a reserve Chaplain with the USAF, I thought perhaps her husband was in the military, ...maybe on a Temporary Duty Assignment somewhere. Surely, such a marvelous lady would not be without a man!

Planning to leave the area for a while, I decided I must find out whether or not she was engaged or married, or otherwise committed to someone. At the close of a church service, I went up to her and asked, "Do you have a husband?"

She answered simply, "No." "Would you like to have one?" I mumbled cautiously.

"Yes." was her unequivocal answer.

With such a clear, unambiguous, and unmistakable answer, I blurted out "Could we talk about it?"

She agreed and gave me a telephone number. I waited two weeks and evaluated my emotions. Surely such a lovely lady was without a man for some good reason. Was she flawed in some way? Was she some religious fanatic? Was she a female iceberg who just didn't like men?

I was reluctant to marry again, not wanting to give up my newly discovered independence and peace of mind. After the "Do you have a husband?" episode, I waited patiently for two weeks, and called her. It was Halloween night - not a very romantic night to call a lady, but it was now or never. She answered, but told me she couldn't talk because her parents were visiting.

Well, that is that, I thought. I didn't understand how her parents being present could make a difference. Was she under their thumb? Was that the reason she didn't have a man? Such Thoughts tumbled through my brain as I pondered my next move. I decided to give her my telephone number and told her to call when she had time to talk; Thinking... I will never hear from her again. No wonder she is not married?

"Who was that on the phone?" Gail's mother asked. "Dr. Hollis Green," she replied. At this her father, the Reverend Henry M. Parks, spoke up with an affirmation: "If Dr. Green is calling Gail, it's O.K., I know him through his books; he is a good man."

Then my phone rang! Who could be calling me on Halloween night? Gail returned my call and we arranged to meet for brunch the next day since I was leaving town for several weeks. The rest is history! Well, it is our history, but few know about the facts of this special relationship and marriage.

When I returned from my trip, my heart was pounding with anticipation; I purchased a friendship ring to show my level of interest. We met several times before I had the courage to give her the ring, but nothing prepared me for one little "word" she spoke softly; that one word was "when."

During this first serious conversation, she said, "When we get married, I'll be good to you. When we get married, my love will always be true." That one word, "when," has been a key to my happiness these many years.

A few months later, we decided to get married. Before this was to happen, I wanted to get one understanding in place: it is normal for people in a relationship to get upset, but..."We must never both be upset at the same time!" On February 8, 1974, we were married. That simple, but crucial relationship imperative has created a healthy and spiritual marriage. Just to remember, with thanksgiving, that Providence brought us together, is to create a cohesiveness that enhances our time together.

How could one word, and one person, make such a difference in the life of a man? That is one of the great mysteries of life! That first question began a beautiful friendship that grew into a sweet companionship, and developed into a spiritual fellowship. God is good! With marriages falling apart all around us, it is good to understand that marriage can work. Provided the relationship has a sound foundation in faith, an understanding of roles, solemn agreements, and respect... yes, respect. This is the key to marriage!

39. RESPECT

Do you know what "respect" means?   Let me share with you an incident that will explain the true meaning of "respect" and open the door to a better relationship. Eating lunch with friends in a local restaurant, a young man approached: "Dr. Green, do you ever counsel married couples?" "Occasionally, I do." "Could my wife and I come and talk with you?"

The session was arranged and both came, but both seemed somewhat reluctant to speak. I asked them to write down what they wanted the other to change and place it in an envelope.

This they did. I opened the wife's envelope and read the list and handed it to the husband.   "Read the first one." "I want him to respect me." "What does she mean?" I asked. "I don't have a clue." Outside this room is a large unabridged dictionary on a stand. "Go look up the word 'respect' " I instructed. Returning with a look of consternation, he was asked to share the meaning. "It means 'to look at, to pay attention to.' "

"Do you understand what she wants?" "If you mean, do I understand her statement, 'I want him to respect me.' "Yes, that is what I mean." "Yes, I believe I understand the problem; she wants me to look at her and pay attention to her."

"Are you willing to do that?" "Yes!" Case closed!

Reconciliation was complete, a child was born. So a vital key to happiness in marriage is simply the little word, "respect – to look at, to pay attention to..." If there is shared respect in a relationship, both will receive the attention and appreciation required to maintain a mutual friendship and a workable marriage.

Since I have shared the key word "respect" let me go further and say that this little word is the secret to building a "better spouse trap" and the master key needed to make marriage a mutual admiration society.

40. OPPORTUNITY AND OBLIGATION FOR CHANGE

Communities in a Pluralistic Society -- All communities in a pluralistic society are a mixing bowl of various cultures and traditions. Each person in the community has both the opportunity and obligation to effect positive social change. Each opening for constructive change requires action. There are occasions in most communities to produce positive social change and moral progress; therefore, it becomes an obligation for all concerned to work toward such progress and transformation of their community. This is particularly incumbent on community leadership to see that the mixing bowl does not become a simmering stew pot of festering frustration.

Social Change Requires a Mixing -- Social change may require the mixing of community traditions and cultures. By adding some aspect of one culture to another, the assimilation produces common ground for change. The combination of traditions produces transformation and adjustments to both thought and process. As change is assimilated, answers are worked out in advance of anticipated questions and a positive attitude for interaction becomes a dynamic policy for action. This tactic produces a strategy for positive change as individuals adjust to the differences around them. The ability to accommodate and adjust to a new environment or a larger association is a noble and valued aspect of human nature. In fact, this is what makes the world go around or at least move forward toward common ground known as social progress.

Many Approaches to Social Change -- There are as many approaches to social change as there are citizens. As individuals function within a given culture or tradition, they constantly seek to maintain the major aspects of customs but are willing to accept incremental steps toward both intellectual and social change. There is an automatic reaching for a new and different way; an ambitious striving toward different and higher goals. Of course, there are restraining forces that obstruct such progress. The restraints that prevent progress come in the forms of persons, traditions, and certain aspects of culture: food, clothing, music, religion, politics, and personal and social distance. As one matures in social graces, they become willing to overlook traditional and cultural warnings and navigate and at times negotiate both social and personal distance to better understand their neighbors. It is this course of action that facilitates positive social change.

Tainted by the Moral Deficiencies -- In the process of social change there is concern that one does not become tainted by the moral deficiencies of the other culture, tradition or individual behavior. It is in this regard that one must be vigilant, willing to take a cautious look at other cultures and traditions, but to also be discerning and accept only those aspects of the other culture or tradition that does not violate their moral standard and personal behavior. The intention is to allow good to overcome evil rather than to sanction immoral behavior. Should one accept the dishonorable aspects of a culture or tradition and attempt to imitate shameful behavior, a progressive debauchery establishes a slippery slope toward evil that produces deterioration and decline in the moral values and meaningful traditions of the community.

On Guard against Moral Decline -- All citizens must be on guard against moral decline that ultimately blocks all constructive change. The process of integration however is designed to make whole or new by adding or bringing together different parts. The study of theology and/or philosophy creates ones value system and ideology. At the level of ideology and values, different individuals and divergent groups find common ground to effect social change in society. This takes place as a formation in the affective domain where ideas of an individual or class are derived exclusively through feelings.

The Affective Domain -- Since feelings can be deceptive, the affective domain must be balanced with a basic philosophy through a study of the processes governing thought and conduct including aesthetics, ethics, logic, metaphysics, morals, character and behavior. This combined with a morsel of theology that considers the relationship between the Divine and the universe as to matters of faith and behavior. The study of theology and/ or philosophy creates ones value system and ideology. At the level of ideology and values, different individuals and divergent groups find common ground to effect social change.

Ideology and the Affective Domain -- Ideology is a formation in the affective domain where ideas of an individual or class are derived exclusively through feelings. Consequently, one must be aware that all aspects of integration and social change are emotional and may be disturbing and at times troubling. However, the need for social progress and moral development demands that efforts be made to effect constructive social change. The big question: will the community be better after this change?

King's Non-violent Approach -- At the death of Martin Luther King, Jr. others found a list on his desk of 200 men most interested in Civil Rights in the South. My name was on that list. As a clergy/educator, it pleased me that someone of another race had recognized my interest in equality and justice. It was firmly believed that social change could be effected without political upheaval; that real progress could be made in integration without the rancor and animosity of politics. King's non-violent approach was of interest to me and it initiated a process that developed several social constructs about change.

The Practice of Intentionality -- Social Change is a deliberate and planned process. Yet there are factors that hinder positive progress. The American and English driving practice is a good example of a difference in understanding the left and right. Americans drive on the right side; the English drive on the "correct" side. Another example would be the word "momentarily." For an American the word means "in a moment" for the English the word means "for a moment." Should the Airline Pilot say, "We will be taken off momentarily" the meaning may be understood differently. The same seems to be true for some of the political language in America. Some are on the "left" and others on the "right."

What does "left and right' teach us? -- Being a clergy/educator, a normal approach would be to go to the original language of the New Testament (Greek) to understand left and right. Matthew 6:3 explained in alms giving "don't let the left hand know what the right had is doing." And Luke 23:33 the thieves were placed on either side of Jesus; "one on the right hand, and the other on the left." This supports that charity gifts should be done in secret and when it comes to politics there are criminals on both sides and the "good" is in the middle. For left the Greek used *aristeros* meaning "second best" and for the right *dexios* meaning "dexterity or right side." The left was the side less used and the right had dexterity that cannot be acquired without much practice and experience. So what does the "left and right" teach us? Probably nothing; the good is somewhere in the middle with bad forces on both sides. This is why a moral renaissance is needed.

Understanding "we" and "me" -- Consider your left hand and your right hand. The left hand is "we" and the right hand is "me." The ring finger is on the left hand in Western culture; therefore, the wedding band is normally worn on the left hand because it signifies a relationship with another. Whether it is politics – left and right, or social or spiritual change, the difference can be explained in terms of "we – the group" or "me – the individual." Social change and positive integration will take place at the individual level first; then it can proceed to the groups and the community.

Personal Affirmative Attitude -- What is needed is not only affirmative action, but a personal affirmative attitude. An affirmative attitude may be contrasted with affirmative action. The legal action is a group "we" process while an affirmative attitude is an individual "me" act of behavior. An affirmative attitude is open-minded and offers a way to deal with diversity; it has an open-endedness, which emphasizes responsiveness. An affirmative attitude is simply the practice of intentionality that issues from one's attitude or predisposition to act. The concern is not just believing in a political or social theory, but behaving in a personal way to effect change. While affirmative action is a more corporate or group approach to community or social change, affirmative attitude is individual behavior.

Positive Social Change -- Political and social change normally comes from group or cooperative action, while moral and spiritual change is an individual and personal matter. Groups are not drastically changed as a whole. The renaissance experience is a personal and at times a traumatic or life changing event. Social change is a group process and affirmative attitude is the correct or proper behavior at an individual level. Positive change must begin with the individuals involved in the community.

Objectives of Social Change -- After many years of traveling, teaching, and speaking on the need for intellectual advancement and constructive social change, a friend recommended that a book be written to describe a strategy for social change. The objectives of this book were: (1) Establish a rationale for constructive social change. (2) Value the various aspects of community life. (3) View America in cultural clothes. (4) Distinguish between faith-based thinking and ideology. (5) Develop needs fulfillment in group interaction. (6) See how human needs (psychological, moral, social, and intellectual) are fulfilled by social interaction. And (7) Discovering how moral nurturing is essential to advancing a constructive agenda for positive social change.

The challenge: to preserve the original character of the community while respectfully enhancing the potential progress of the community taking into account all the varied aspects of culture and tradition. Individuals change more rapidly than groups and groups change easier than communities. Consequently, the strategy must be to affect change at the individual level so that changed individuals can produce change in the groups of which they are a part. Then a combination of changed groups can generate change in the community.

41. LIKE FOOTSTEPS EACH CHILD IS DIFFERENT

If the old adage be true that the hand that rocks the cradle rules the world; then those who guide the footsteps of growing children will be building the Kingdom of Heaven. It was the Master Himself who said, "Permit the children to come to me, and do not hinder them: for of such is the kingdom of God." (Luke 18:16 EDNT) Since ancient scripture was clear that training up children in the proper way would provide assurance that when they are older they would not depart from such guidance. All that is needed is a well-trained hand to rock that cradle, and eventually point those wandering feet in the right direction.

Custodial childcare is not a basket of bad apples that need to be culled from society. Rather it is a cradle of socialization filled with precious fruit of the womb picked prematurely from the tree of life to prevent further deterioration. Just like footprints, each child is different and age-specific care is required to preserve them for a positive future. Certainly the children have their share of trouble and need a happy place to enjoy food, fun, and friends.

It is reported that Mark Twain once said, "Laughter is the Hand of God on troubled world." An ancient proverb dealt with both sides of this issue, "A merry heart does good like a medicine, but a broken spirit dries the bones. (Proverbs 17:22) This is a noble goal. The challenging arena of custodial care is filled with committed service providers who not only supply remedial and surrogate parenting, but the best of them do so in an atmosphere of laughter; applying the medicine of a merry heart to the dry bones and broken spirit of disadvantaged children.

42. ATTITUDE, KNOWLEDGE, AND BEHAVIOR

There is a relationship between the attitude, knowledge, and behavior of caregivers in remedial and surrogate parenting and the quality of custodial care for abused, neglected, or abandoned children. Everyone involved in childcare must make an effort to assure a positive and professional attitude in custodial care staff, to provide sufficient knowledge of remedial development, and to provide basic guidance as to personal and professional behavior necessary to make surrogate parenting work with needy children in the custodial arena. There is great need for personnel working in

Childcare facilities, orphanages, and foster parents to pick up the slack in society when custodial care is not sufficient or agencies of government are slow to respond to the needs of disadvantaged children.

43. OBJECTIVES
FOR A CUSTODIAL CARE FACILITY

1.   Create a home environment conducive to learning that promotes growth, mutual respect and trust among children and caregivers.

2.   Structure childcare programs to educate and develop children giving priority to behavioral and learning needs of disadvantaged children.

3.   Provide structures, learning resources, technology and processes designed to motivate and engage children in learning activities of development to prepare them for the real world of work and family.

4.   Develop a tutoring/learning process that permits self-directed, individualized, face-to-face, and classroom learning in real life situations with dialog/support systems and technology suitable for disadvantaged children.

5.   Strive for multicultural awareness with a broad exchange of teaching/learning experience across cultural and ethnic boundaries.

6.   Partner with business and industry to produce meaningful programs for childcare and development in regions of need.

7.   Work with the Government and Child Protection Agencies to establish quality childcare facilities and train qualified childcare workers and staff.

Negative Conditioning -- The road to custodial care is paved with good intentions and negative conditioning. Some see the problem and do nothing. Others recognize the difficulty and do little. Still others see the impact of a dysfunctional family on the children and build a bridge of hope. When children walk across the bridge of hope they find a safe village where they can live and grow. But negative conditioning in the previous environment becomes a formidable barrier to remedial and surrogate parenting in the custodial arena. This must be understood to accomplish the process of remedial development in special needs children. Negative conditioning and procrastination are also problems for those providing custodial care; past occurrences in their own life are sometimes projected on the child. Surrogate parenting or child-rearing requires special skills, qualities, experience, and responsibilities to teach and care for a child in a safe environment. Procrastination denies or delays positive action and permits the previous negative conditioning to fester and aggravate the positive aspects of custodial care. It would be helpful for custodial workers to understand the meaning of key words used in the book to establish the structure and parameters of childcare in the custodial arena.

Operational Definition for Key Terms

Abandoned – the abdication of personal responsibility for a child left behind for others to provide care and support.

Abused – the physical, psychological, or sexual maltreatment of a child including all illegal, improper, or harmful practices.

Attitude – the predisposition to act in a negative or positive manner in a given situation and a tendency to respond in a given way to agent or factor that provokes interest or response.

Behavior – the way one responds to a specific set of conditions that produces goal-directed activity of the caregiver and the child.

Child – a young human being between birth and puberty.

Custodial – relating to the legal custody of and responsibility for a child's nurturing and guardianship.

Knowledge – the level of familiarity with the facts about both the child and the process of remedial and surrogate parenting.

Neglected – to fail to receive the proper or required care and attention to a child because of carelessness, inability, or indifference.

Parenting – the experiences, skills, qualities, and responsibilities involved in being a legal guardian and in teaching and/or caring for a child.

Remedial – acting as a remedy or solution to a child's problem.

Surrogate –taking the place of another as a substitute or replacement.

44. AN ACROSTIC OF LOVE

LOVE IS: learning, opening, viewing, enjoying.

L -- **Learning** from the past;

O -- **Opening** your heart to someone;

V -- **Viewing** the future with confidence;

E -- **Enjoying** the present moment.

45. A RELATIONAL DOCUMENT

The New Testament is a relational document designed to guide believers in their relationship with God and their behavior toward others. The EVERGREEN Devotional New Testament (EDNT) contains narratives about the life of Jesus, letters to Theophilus, letters to believers in churches, relational letters, and letters to scattered believers. These letters with relational value are presented together. Also, the nature of early converts, scattered throughout the known world without a local assembly to mother their faith, appears to be similar to the mobility of the present pluralistic society. Away from family and friends, moving from job to job and town to town, many believers are without a congregation home to nurture their faith. There is an urgent need for a devotional text that is true to the original manuscripts but is easy to read. Hopefully, the Devotional New Testament will meet part of this need.

Relational and Inductive Study -- Combining aspects of relational and inductive study produced the concept of a Devotional New Testament. Holy Scripture means exactly what the first person who heard it understood it to mean, not what culture, tradition, or translators interpret the words to mean. Because most translations and versions of scripture are academic with copious notes that slow the reader and hinder the devotional value. Getting a sense of the original intent provides an improved understanding of the inspired text. A simple word study comparison between common Greek, Latin syntax and the language used in the KJV can clarify the actual meaning of words and produce a devotional understanding.

Mostly Pristine Issues -- Although the New Testament deals with pristine issues, the basic concepts and constructs deal with a group of Christians scattered because of persecution. Without Christian assemblies converts continued to attend Jewish synagogues. Some of the synagogues were more Christian than Jewish, such as the one in Berea, but most remained bound to the old system. These letters were designed to assist both with the scattered nature of the believers without home assembly support and struggling new congregations with little knowledge of the Christian faith.

The Books and NT Letters have a Chronology -- The New testament was given in books and is best understood by books. The text also has a chronology. If one accepts the concept of logical development, then reading the books in some chronological order would make sense. The books of the New Testament were written to individuals, scattered believers, and assembled believers in particular places and times. The context of these facts assists in understanding the purpose and meaning of a given book or letter. Certainly seeing the order and nature of God's revelation at various times informs a clearer understanding of the meaning of scripture. God does stack His revelation "line upon line, and precept upon precept." Although the books are presented in groups according to theme and addressees, they are chronological by book within these groups.

Use Original Language to Develop Dogma -- The devotional text does no violence to the original language because it is based on common Greek and common word meanings. Hopefully, it is objective and that personal feelings are excluded. The work is designed to make scripture clear to the devotional reader. Doctrine should be formed only from a clear understanding of the original languages, not an English translation. This text is designed for devotional reading. Academics, theologians, and Biblical scholars should themselves use the original Greek of the New Testament to develop and defend specific teachings or dogma.

The Pristine Experience was Relational -- The New Testament is relational and when personal and interpersonal relationships are properly ordered there is less need for instruction in doctrine. One should remember that the New Testament congregations did not have a New Testament. Some parts of the Old Testament were available through the Jewish traditions, but the Gentile converts did not yet have a New Testament. A few letters were circulated from assembly to assembly, but the collection of books and letters as we know them were not available. Primarily the pristine believers were concerned about a redemptive relationship with Christ and a proper relationship with others. This is what made them Christian; not the existence of sacred writings. Devotional reading of scripture is instructive as to belief and behavior.

> *All scripture will provide instruction in righteousness: All sacred writings are God-breathed, and serviceable for teaching, for warning, for correction, for instruction in righteousness, in order that the man of God may be adequately equipped, for every good work.* (2 Timothy 3:16, 17 EDNT)

A Candid Rendering of a Passage -- Through the years in preparation to preach or teach a candid rendering of the New Testament passage was made to frame my thinking. To arrive at the original intent of scripture was the goal. Using key words in the 1611 KJV diligently compared with Koine Greek, Latin syntax and common usage, a straightforward rendering was made. It was assumed that God did not intend the Bible to be interpreted by academics, theologians, or even preachers. To follow a New Testament model, originally scripture was read publicly to the congregation without explanation and passed on to another congregation. There was no effort to examine and describe the grammar of a sentence or a particular word in a sentence because the congregation understood the common language. There were no "read along" texts available. The congregation listened and understood.

The Devotional New Testament is an effort to place scripture into a more understandable language. The work may not demonstrate a rigid scholarship as would a word for word translation of the text.

This is because the Greek word order and many of the explanations for translating a passage differently than other existing texts are so academic that the explanations hinder the devotional value of reading scripture. Some may think it too sermonic, but this work seeks to be devotional, not strictly scholarly. The objective was to make the text clear and understandable to the average reader the same way a pastor attempts to present scripture from the pulpit. This EDNT is a candid rendering of my objective understanding of the text.

Speaking at the Religious Emphasis Week at a college where my mother was a Dean, concern gripped me because it was one of the few times my mother had heard me speak. It had been my style to first understand the passage of scripture and then transliterate it as simply as possible using common language. Normally, my approach was "The deeper meaning here is...or the original intent of the language here means, etc." As the first service progressed mother turned to a colleague and said, "He will say things that are not in your Bible, but he is a good and honest man." As I transliterated certain words and gave my free rendering, mother turned to her friend and said, "See I told you he would say things that are not in your Bible." Yet, the Greek Professor shared with his class, "Listen in chapel and you will understand how the study of Greek is to assist your understanding of the language and not to demonstrate your knowledge." When the Professor told me his statement to the class, I was encouraged to continue the process of giving the devotional meaning of scripture in my public ministry.

Relational and Inductive Study Combined

-- Colleagues have encouraged me to make these practical interpretations available and they are presented in the EDNT as an explanation of how the candid rendering of the New Testament was reached and presented as a devotional text. It is a combination of both relational study and inductive study together with an understanding of the original language. Relational study requires one to listen, reflect, connect and act often in a subjective manner. Inductive study involves more objectivity and scholarship. Both processes have value, but need to be combined to be effective. By bringing together the basic aspects of relational and inductive study, one develops a less emotional and more intellectual approach to devotional study. A good identity for this process is a Devotional New Testament.

Both study plans have limitations. In a relational study one reads into the scripture subjectively "personal stuff" that can skew the actual meaning of the words. Inductive study requires one to be more scholarly and "read out of" the text objectively. The difficulty here is the meaning of words. Are the words colored by personal emotions or was the meaning objectively obtained. Although relational study is built on a personal relationship with God and an understanding that the study is intended to nurture and enhance this relationship, one is often left to personal devices. Inductive study requires more academic preparation to do the work effectively. Both plans use the basic steps of observation, interpretation and application in the form of three questions: What does the verse say? What does the verse mean? How does the meaning apply to me? Although there is no private interpretation of scripture, there is value in internalizing the meaning, provided it is the true meaning. This is the value of devotional reading.

In relational study the emotions and personal circumstance affect the study. Inductive study places value on sound biblical scholarship and intellectual study. The meaning of words is important and can be life-changing. If one does not know the Greek language (a process that can take up to twenty years to accomplish) then the recommendation is to use an Unabridged English Dictionary (UED) to obtain the actual meaning of KJV words at the time they were selected in 1611 and placed in the translation. Using an UED can assist in digging out the meaning of words. One cannot truly apply the meaning unless the true meaning of words has been determined.

A Repository of Classical Knowledge -- There must be a proper worshipful approach to the study of Holy Scripture. Honest and effective study requires a level of scholarship that is not readily available. This is why the Unabridged English Dictionary is recommended. There are only a few classical scholars left in the world. The unabridged dictionary is a repository of much of the classical knowledge of the past and can be an effective tool in examining the ideas and words of an ancient text. Also, with reference to the King James Version it is helpful to understand the meaning of words at the time of the translation. This will lead to a meaning closer to the original intent of scripture. Such an interpretation brings about objective conclusions and meaningful application to life. Devotional study uses aspects of both the relational and inductive plans.

Hearing One Side of a Two-sided Conversation The New Testament is both books and letters written to specific groups or individuals because of specific situations. Understanding a letter is the most difficult. It is similar to hearing one side of a two-sided conversation. One does not clearly know the person or persons to whom the letter was written. Not only is there difficulty in the technical language of New Testament letters; there is the problem of always knowing exactly what prompted the letter or what was the question or letter that was being answered. Therefore, as one interprets sacred scripture there is a dual problem: the technical language of the text and the meaning as understood by the original reader or hearer. Of course the reason for, nature of, and exact situation the letter addresses compounds the difficulty. Written scripture was commonly understood because the language was in the dialect or vernacular of the people.

It would be good to remember that at the Feast of Pentecost when the Holy Spirit gave believers the ability to articulate an unnaturally acquired language. This was done to present "the wonderful works of God in the native language of the people." Since this happened, it points to God's intentionality for sacred writings. The writers were to present the Gospel and sacred writings in a common language that all could understand. Apostle Paul was a multilingual person who adapted his message to the native language of the people. This was true when he wrote letters and when he spoke to people. This is the rationale behind the rendering of the EVERGREEN Devotional New Testament (EDNT).

Most translations and versions are so abstract and footnoted they are not useful for devotional reading. One friend characterized the normal process as being "So academically minded there is little spiritual value." The Word of God was not intended to be filtered through the minds of scholars and theologians; it was to be read directly to the people to whom it was written. The Bible actually means what the first persons who heard it understood it to mean. With translations and versions of the Bible, the meaning is often hidden in the choice of words and the actual meaning of the words in the English language at the time of the rendering. With 60 years of ministry and academic leadership, a lesson of simplicity was learned. The intent is communication not sophistication or complication.

The Lapse of Time -- A difficulty in Bible study is the lapse of time and the translations from one language and culture to another. Research has demonstrated that when one translates something from one language, culture, or time period to another, the meaning changes. Since there are no copies of the original documents of the Bible in the handwriting of the writer, and since most of us are not classical scholars who know the nuances of many languages, the best we can do is to understand the reason for word selection or language choice by the selected classical scholars authorized to translate the Bible.

Roots of the English Language -- One problem understanding the English versions of scripture, is the language itself. The present English language originated in the Indo-European region and what is now Modern English developed in Western German vernacular, then into Low German parlance, and finally into Old English (450-1150), then Middle English (1150-1475) and finally into Modern English. In 1611 at the time of the translation of the King James Version of the Bible, English was acquiring its modern external form, but English scholars were still using subordination of clauses as a primary aspect of language.

Subordination in old grammar designated a clause that was dependent on another clause that did not itself constitute a formal sentence. A subordinate clause—also called a **dependent clause**—begins with a **subordinate conjunction** or a **relative pronoun** and contains both a **subject** and a **verb**. This combination of words does **not** form a **complete sentence**. It will instead require a reader to add additional information to finish the thought. Such clauses were introduce by subordinate conjunctions: after, although, as, because, before, even, if, even though, in order that, once, provided that, rather than, since, so that, that, though, than, unless, until, when, whenever, where, whereas, wherever, whether, while, why; or relative pronouns: that, which, whichever, who, whoever, whom, whose, whosoever, or whomever. This linking of a subordinate clause to a main clause complicates the understanding of the modern English language reader.

The old grammar defined a sentence as "One idea fully developed." This is now the definition of a Standard English paragraph. This is another reason reading the Scripture in the verse format places long sentences with multiple subordination (using colons; semi-colons, commas, etc.). Most of the more recent versions of the Bible make paragraphs out of these long sentences. Since a paragraph is now one idea fully developed, a reader of scripture should attempt to determine the "main idea" in each expository unit and not use a subordinate clause, which supports the main idea, to develop doctrine.

During the intervening years, the English language accepted thousands of new words and refined the meaning of others; consequently, it is difficult to actually know what a present word meant several hundred years ago. For this reason, the New Testament presented here is divided into paragraphs for reading and study. A look at how the King James Bible came to be would assist the understanding of the language and the process involved.

The Canonical Order of the New Testament -- The canonical order of the manuscript in the original KJV (1611) was 49 books divided into seven divisions. The Old Testament contained: (1) The Law, (2) The Prophets, and (3) The Writings. The New Testament contained: (4) The Gospels and Acts, (5) The General Epistles, (6) The Epistles of Paul and (7) The Book of Revelation. Early Church fathers altered the order into 66 books presently used in most versions. There have been numerous translations and versions of the original text and some changes in the order of the Old Testament, but the canon of the New Testament has remained the same. There is no credible question about the number (27) of books;

however, these are not in chronological order. The Bible is a book of books written over many generations to show God's dealing with the human race and in particular the body of believers. The Bible forms one continuous story, a kind of string of pearls, strung together with a blood line. It is a progressive unfolding of truth "line upon line, precept upon precept" to form the story of humanity in relation to God. This devotional version places the New Testament books chronologically in order in five groups to show the development over time. It is for this reason that the New Testament books are grouped and then placed in chronological order within the section: Narratives About the Life of Jesus, Letters to Theophilus, Letters to Assembled Believers, Relational Letters, and Letters to Scattered Believers.

Guidance for the Reader -- The reader should be aware of emphasis by position, proportion and punctuation. In composition (com-position) everything has a position or place. If words and phrases are in the right place, the emphasis is clear. Also, provided the punctuation is properly placed, the reader has a better understanding of the text. In addition to the process of subordination discussed before, punctuation can assist or hinder the reader's understanding. The first or last part of a book or chapter has position and the material in the middle needs proportion or more elaboration. Punctuation is the key to understanding.

Punctuation is similar to traffic signals. Some indicate full stop while others warn drivers to slow down, be cautious, or provide instruction or guidance. The eye cannot see when it is moving; it must focus. Punctuation stops the eye and places words or phrases in the emphatic position.

This is why punctuation is important. A brief review of English grammar punctuation could assist the reader.

> A sentence ends with a period [.] (full stop); a question mark [?] suggests an interrogatory remark or inquiry; an exclamation point [!] suggest excitement or emphasis. The semicolon [;] separates two related but independent clauses or a complex series of items that contain commas. A colon [:] introduces a list or denotes that additional information follows. The dash [-] makes a brief interruption within a statement, a sudden change of thought, an additional comment, a dramatic qualification, or to add a parenthetical statement for clarification but still relevant to the central idea. Use the comma [,] to denote that words or phrases refer to the same person or thing, or to show a break within a sentence that adds information or develops the central idea.

The New Testament originally, written in common Greek, did not have chapters, verses, or punctuation. The language itself clearly placed words and phrases together and in positions of emphasis.

Books and letters were later divided into chapters and verses for readers to search and find particular information. The translators also added punctuations based on the placement of the words or phrases. Most translations and renderings of the New Testament capitalized the first word of each verse even if it did not start a new sentence. This confuses the English reader and causes one to give prominence and worth to subordinate thoughts rather than value the main idea. Consequently, the Evergreen EDNT does not always capitalize the beginning word of a new verse unless there is a terminal punctuation before the verse number. The new verse should be read as a continuation of the previous thought or additional development supporting the central idea of the paragraph. Also, instead of quotation marks, the EDNT uses a Capital letter to begin a quotation. The EDNT has attempted to capitalize the pronouns that refer to the Trinity. Since the KJV had so many pronouns; hopefully, this will clarify the He, Him, His, referring to the Godhead and make it easier for the reader to attribute value to the antecedent.

46. A THEOLOGY OF THE DISADVANTAGED

With conversion to Christianity as an adult, Subesh Ramjattan brought with him a varied history. His life narrative included growing up poor, with limited opportunities, educational struggles, early illness that included the loss of a kidney, the death of a younger brother, business problems, the use of alcohol, and marriage difficulties, contribute to his development of a theology of the disadvantaged. This background together with the New Testament picture of a loving and caring Jesus produced a "Subesh" version of God's concern for the disadvantaged.

Jesus cared for the little children and demonstrated concern for the poor. He healed the sick, wept at the death of a friend, loved His enemies, took the long view of life, and planned carefully for a legacy of followers to continue His work. This appears to inform the theology of the disadvantaged utilized in the work and ministry of Subesh and his wife, Debra. According to the book, The Anapausis Partnership (2011), ---Debra Ramjattan shared a common background experience and this informs her support for their work and ministry together.

This theology of the disadvantaged has produced, the Bridge of Hope, a safe place for abused, abandoned, and disadvantaged children to grow, develop and bloom into productive citizens. This theology produced the Anapausis Community to service people of faith in their search for a better life, improved relationships, and ministry. The ministry includes a "quality of life" component shared with couples and individuals struggling with the normal adult difficulties and relationship issues in business and married life. The capstone of this ministry is a four-stage project to serve the needs of the Elderly in Trinidad and Tobago. This is indeed a theology of the disadvantaged with the goal of improving the quality of life for all.

The right theology is a key ingredient of "vision" for a leader in ministry. There must be a balance between affluence and compassion. Wealth or what some call "prosperity" provides the means to be compassionate toward the less fortunate, but without spiritual vision the effort to truly serve others will fail. Doing what is right for the poor and disadvantaged only to avoid leaving them behind, is not sufficient to empower them with hope, opportunity, and promise for the future. A true leader must look beyond the present and see possibilities. This was a reason for the writer of Proverbs to pen, "Where there is no vision, the people perish." (Proverbs 29:18 KJV) That reason seems clear: without a balanced theology and a working philosophy, the ingredient of vision will be missing in leadership and the people will suffer.

There is a classic line by Shakespeare, written for Brutus in <u>Julius Caesar</u>, that speaks to an understanding of this proverb: "There is a tide in the affairs of men, which, taken at the flood, leads on to fortune; omitted, all the

voyage of their life is bound in shallows and in miseries..."
When vision flows from the soul and overflows the heart
into the hands of the leader, the people including the
poor are blessed. It appears that Subesh Ramjattan has
manifested the key ingredients of spiritual leadership in his
ministry to the disadvantaged.

His books are a message to believers of the Christian
faith to encourage their participation in the Commission of
Christ and develop a life-style of witness and care for the
disadvantaged. All believers going about their daily lives
must make disciples and then nurture them in the faith
until the converts become both a meaningful home builder
and a missionary in the marketplace sharing their witness of
saving grace.

47. NAVIGATING THE CHALLENGES OF FAITH-BASED BEHAVIOR

**There are many comparisons between the old
sailing ships** and the early songs about the Old Gospel
Ship. The sailing ships had rules to secure an adequate crew
and safe passage for both ship and cargo. An individual
boards the Ship of Zion by invitation, conversion and
contract with the Captain. The knowledge-based behavior
of Christian converts has similarities with the regulations
governing aboard ship conduct and cooperation among the
crew. Not only must working sailors know and understand
the rules of conduct and operation; they must behave
according to the rules or suffer personal consequence and
bring great risk to the crew and the ship. This is also true of
the faith-based behavior of believers.

The Captain of the ship had total authority aboard a sailing ship and each sailor must follow the guidance of the Captain without question. Failure to follow the rules or obey clear and fixed guidelines created difficult times for all concerned. It was the task of the older crew members to teach, train, and guide, the behavior of the younger members. This is also the task of the senior members of the Christian faith. They are responsible to both exhibit and instruct faith-based behavior to the next generation.

There exists a companionship and solidarity of mission among the crew of a sailing ship. Camaraderie among the crew was essential to a safe journey for crew, cargo, and all passengers. There is also an expectation of fellowship and companionship among those who follow Jesus, the Captain of the Old Gospel Ship. This speaks to the company of believers traveling together. They are a "fellowship of believers" traveling together on the same ship. When one individual fails to carry out the proper behavior, other individuals suffer difficulty and the faith-based mission suffers loss. Consequently, the band of believers are accountable to each other and ultimately to the Helmsman of the Ship.

The modern world has lost many of the lessons from the seafaring era. Most social and faith-based leaders are far from the seafaring age and the concept of "helmsman" escapes their vocabulary. There are many definitions of cybernetics and this is a problem for a faith-based understanding. The original intent of the word is lost in the input of various ideas into working definitions to fit a particular personal field of interest. Cybernetics treats not things but ways of behaving. It does not ask "what is this thing?" but "what does it do?" and "what can it do?" An understanding of this definition would bring us back to the original intent of cybernetics: "a helmsman who steers the ship." Modern man has imposed multiple definitions on many words that have value to people of faith. That is the reason for structuring this book around a sailing ship in the seafaring era to review the process of getting crew and cargo to a safe harbor.

The term "helmsman" comes from the Greek word, *kybernētēs*, and is translated as "cybernetics" which misses the original meaning of steering a ship. The helmsman was the one who guided the course of the ship and understood both the workings of the ship, the currents, the winds, and the nature of the waters in which the ship was sailing. The Helmsman of the Old Gospel Ship is clearly Jesus and those who presume to follow His leadership must accept as His words of invitation and faithfully follow the written guidance in the preserved Sacred Writings.

With these concepts and constructs in mind, those who accept the invitation to board the Ship of Zion are converted from their old life and established in a moral lifestyle. Lifestyle is a word from sociology meaning the way a person lives; it suggests a style of living that reflects the attitudes and values of a person. To establish a moral lifestyle one must both believe and behave the clear concepts presented in the preserved Sacred Writings. This lifestyle both honors the historical past and changes those who observe the proper conduct of believers. Change comes to others when they encounter the fervent witness of those blessed by the power of a divine invitation.

> 27. While He spoke, a woman in the crowd, with a loud voice said, Blessed is the Mother who birthed you and nursed you .28. But Jesus said, Rather

blessed are those who hear the word of God and behave it (Luke 11:27-28 EDNT).

The sailing guidelines passed on by skilled seamen and officers became a working contract for new seamen to keep the ship afloat and the crew safe. The crew of a sailing ship beside the officers included: cabin boys sent to sea to learn the ropes and the maritime trade and carpenters who kept the ship afloat and made necessary repairs. Good crew members were of great value to a sailing ship. This is equally true of individuals whose faith-based contract places them in a responsible position of moral leadership and faithful service for the benefit of others.

The lack of moral lifestyle among some in faith-based groups is troubling. Bad behavior diminishes the testimony of the faithful, as much as, a leak below the water line of a ship. Being a part of the fellowship of believers requires everyone to follow the rules. When anyone fails in this area of responsibility, the whole community suffers. This is similar to a crew member of a sailing ship failing to perform vital duties that endangers the ship, the cargo and the crew.

Normally, a new believer is willing to follow the rules and the spiritual guidance of a respected leader. An example o this behavior is a new convert in Hong Kong who wrote his mother in mainland China "I am now reading the Bible and behaving it." He had the right idea. Conversion is supposed to regenerate the soul and redirect the priorities of daily life. According to Scripture, conversion is to produce a new creation that generates a revitalized soul that brings into being a moral witness. We need more converts who read, believe and clearly behave preserved Sacred Writings.

The preserved Word makes this fact clear:

*17. Therefore if any man be in Christ, he
is a new creation: observe, the old things
have passed away; all things have become
new. 18. All things are of God, who has
brought us together in Himself by Jesus
Christ, and has given to us the ministry of
bringing people together; 19. how that God
was in Christ bringing together the world to
Himself, not counting their false steps and
blunders against them; and has committed
us to speak intelligent words that bring man
and God together. 20. Now seeing we are
representatives for Christ, as though God did
make His appeal through us: we implore you
in Christ's stead, come together with God. (2
Corinthians 5:17-20 EDNT)*

The Sacred Covenant charts a course of action to guide
believers on their journey from earth to heaven. It is not
necessary to search for a route or worry about the next
phase of the journey. With confidence in the Helmsman
of the Ship, and the fellowship of other believers, it is just
a matter of following the rules and accepting spiritual
guidance. Sure there will be challenges along the way,
temptations will come that must be resisted, choices must
be made, and other circumstances that could push one
off course, but those difficulties can be dealt with through
simple faith and trust. When one has trust in God and a
covenant alliance with other believers, the behavior for the
journey should be clear. Each thought and act should move
one closer to faith and forward toward the ultimate goal – a
moral lifestyle. A faith-based lifestyle determines both the
course of action, the destination of the journey and provides
a standard of behavior appropriate for one traveling on the

Old Gospel Ship. Come join Subesh Ramjattan on the Ship of Zion sailing toward the eternal shores of Paradise.

48. STEPS TO ACQUIRE A PURPOSE

Walking on the streets of Oxford, England with my oldest son, we saw graffiti scrawled on a college wall *"Life is not a paragraph."* Asking my son what it meant, his answer was clear "A paragraph is an idea fully developed and if you are alive, then you are not fully developed -- so life can't be a paragraph." Well, so much for those words of wisdom. Human development is progress overtime and one must have a guiding purpose to stay on the determined course despite difficulties.

Purpose is considered the long-range reason and the general direction or focus for development. Purpose is always singular, because one cannot travel in two directions at the same time and a double-minded person is unstable. Sufficient to each day are the difficulties that all humans must face. The struggle for a quality of life is to overcome daily difficulties and not be sidetracked from the planned course.

As a young man, I had a motto on my desk *"Ideas are witty little things, but they don't work unless you do!"* Each morning I would think about this adage to get my creative juices flowing. Realizing that everyone had the same 24-hours in a day, I would consider how I could best accomplish the multiple tasks of the day by asking myself three questions: What can I do different? What can I do better? What can I do new? Then when a notion, a thought, or an inspiration hit my brain wave, I would spin it around until it formalized into an "idea" worthy of my time. Perhaps this is why I became a writer: a paragraph is one idea fully developed. Here are my steps to acquire a purpose for the day and establish a long-range direction for life despite the normal difficulties:

- Spin a thought into an idea.
- Plant an idea and reap an action.
- Repeat an action and gain a practice.
- Produce a practice and harvest a lifestyle.
- Achieve a lifestyle and acquire a purpose.

1. Spin a thought into an idea. The paragraphs of life consist of ideas. When ideas are fully developed, your words make sense to you and to others. Developed ideas give life meaning. Ideas do not work by themselves you must work with them to move your life forward. Ideas are curious little things that probe and pry at your intellect and must be planted and nourished to grow. An idea you have today may not work tomorrow. Ideas are short lived.

2. Plant an idea and reap an action. When an idea is firmly planted in the conscious mind, it will nourish deeds, even exploits that provide activities and undertakings that prepare the steps forward to assure advancement on the path toward progress. Often you may have to repeat the process to assure you are on a worthy path. Never neglect the power of replication, because repeating a process opens the mind to areas of concern and possible improvement.

3. Repeat an action and gain a practice. You have heard the saying, "Practice makes perfect." However, I am not sure this is true. It is true that repeating an action will establish a practice, but practice may make it better but will not make things perfect. Almost every concept and construct conceived by the human element has flaws. No mere mortal, not even you, is always right, constantly wonderful, or immaculate. To err is human; therefore, you must always repeat the process to be certain you have found the best way forward. To gain a practice is to develop a process with procedures that minimizes human error and flawed thinking. The classic fields of knowledge were the practice of law, the practice of medicine, and practice of philosophy (that included religion).

The field of law has review by a higher court, medicine has the autopsy to determine malpractice or the cause of death and philosophy has the logic of Boolean algebra to determine the answer of "true or false." Personal behavior has the check and balance known as the human conscience. No process, procedure, or person produces a perfect lifestyle. Life is trial and error!

4. Produce a practice and harvest a lifestyle. Proverbs speaks to this issue *"the breath of man is the candle of the Lord that searches the bottom of the heart"* (Proverbs 20:27 EDOT). It appears that lawyers send their mistakes to prison; medical doctors send their mistakes to the grave; philosophers send their unanswered questions to the abyss of verbosity. Religion practitioners send their mistakes to (well- - - -) -- judgment before the God of the Universe.

5. Achieve a lifestyle and acquire a purpose. Daily activities speak to lifestyle. It is a way of life, an individual routine, or a personal standard of living. It is this routine that determines your purpose in life: your reason for existing. It has to do with intentionality, which is the power of your

mind to produce ideas and stand for values. It
has to do with ideology, a combination of personal
philosophy and theology that determine your
social role(s) and ideas and values. It is at this
combined level of intentionality and ideology that
human beings work together to achieve positive
social progress and purposeful control of their
behavior.

49. AN OPEN DOOR OF OPPORTUNITY

Adversity often becomes an open door of
opportunity for achievement. An old adage about life
stated "It is not what happens in life, but what one does
with what happens that makes a difference in the kind of
person one becomes." A saying attributed to Napoleon
about the hazardous struggle of battle is appropriate here,
"There is a time A story from early television tells of a young
mother who asked an Interviewer "May I say something to
my young son at home?" Given permission, she said "Billy,
whatever you are doing, stop it!" It is natural for all of us to
do things that displease others. The solution: stop it!

In sacred writings we find weak and failing
individuals selected for a great work and this in spite
of their shortcomings. God often choose the young to
confound the wise or the weak to overcome the strong.
When one is divinely touched and called for a cause of
action, qualification is not the issue; it is availability that
counts. There is always enablement for those chosen for a
moral cause. Even the faint of heart are used to accomplish
great things for the good of mankind. Through the power of
forgiveness and divine anointing, individuals are enabled to

make positive achievements because God qualifies those He calls.

The sacred record is filled with individuals who failed at some aspect of their life or disappointed others by their behavior. Adam and Eve made a big blunder in the Garden, but God used them to start the human race. Noah got drunk, but God trusted him to build the Ark that saved the seed family of humanity. Abraham lied about his wife, but God used him to father a Nation. Jonah ran from God, but he was given a divine message for Nineveh. Moses was slow of speech, a stutterer, and had a bad temper, but God gave him the Law and used him to lead Israel out of bondage and servitude. David, the Shepherd Boy, felt unqualified, but God made him King; he then misused his position and power to take another man's life and wife. Surely, there were negative consequences to this behavior, but God still used him greatly.

Gideon was insecure and wanted a large army, but God limited him to a few good men (so God could provide the victory). Thomas was a doubter, but he saw and believed. Peter cursed, lied, and denied the Messiah, but God used him to strengthen others and lead the pristine group of believers. Paul persecuted believers and was struck down on the road to Damascus, but God used him as an Apostle to the Gentiles and trusted him to write one-fourth of the New Testament. Zacchaeus over taxed the poor, but invited Jesus to his house and made restitution. Zacharias and Elizabeth stopped praying for a son, but God enabled them to become elderly parents of John the Baptist who prepared the way for the Messiah. God doesn't always call the qualified, but He always qualifies the called. God desires that believers live a life that is faithful to Him, not strive to be successful in the material world.

It is clear from my life experience that adversity can be overcome. Most of us have experienced what seemed to be impossible circumstances, but in reality they were great opportunities to use lessons learned and move forward. Also, I have learned from family and friends that failure is not the end, but a starting place for better things. Of course, real and lasting achievements do not come without hard work, but hardship and misfortune prepares the mind, body, and spirit of individuals and enables them to overcome future difficulties.

No mountain is too high and no valley too low, but that diligence and perseverance can bring accomplishments. God made both the mountains and the valleys, then man was made from the earth and told to "subdue, conquer, overpower, and overcome" the difficulties he would face. Consequently, mankind throughout the generations learned to surmount difficulties and grow a garden, build a home, raise a family, grow a business, develop a community, and establish Nations. The accumulated wisdom of the ages is preserved for those who wish to achieve their purpose in life.

Napoleon once said "in every battle when both sides have lost --- victory belongs to the one who attacks first after this point of loss." The lesson here was clear, when trouble comes one must take positive action to move past the difficulty. Loss can actually create the opportunity for gain. This common sense lesson from the past is most telling, "Necessity is the mother of invention." Difficulties can become stumbling stones to produce present failure or stepping stones to a positive future.

Faith-based principles can make a difference in a productive life. Starting with the Commandments from the Hebrew Torah and appearing in various forms in the scared writings of most religions, common sense lessons are taught by moral scholars. One such lesson is recognized as a Golden Rule and moral leaders are stewards of both the instructions and the divine resources provided by Providence and preserved in sacred writings. The guidance of this Rule is so basic it is communicated in sacred writing in various forms:

Buddhism –"Hurt not others in ways that you yourself would find hurtful." *(Udana-Vaarga 5,1)*

Christianity –"As you would that men should do unto you, do you also to them likewise." *(Luke 6:31)*

Hinduism – "This is the sum of duty; do naught unto others what you would not have them do unto you." *(Mahabharata 5, 1517)*

Judaism – "What is hateful to you, do not do to your fellowman. This is the entire Law; all the rest is commentary." (Talmud, Shabbat 3id)

Taoism – "Regard your neighbor's gain as your gain, and your neighbor's loss as your own loss." *(Tai Shang Kan Yin P'ien)*

50. CHURCH GROWTH THROUGH NEW CONVERTS AND NEW CONGREGATIONS

Amplifying the Kingdom through Christian celebration and personal worship – *recognizing the "worth-ship of God" in all of life.*

CELEBRATION (Infinity #) Worship

Worship actually means the "worth-ship of God" and is a vertical experience. Worship has little reference to those about; it is a concentration of the divine through prayer, song, witness, and listening to God through the Word. How much is God worth in your life? How do you value God? Worship is observance of Christ's death and resurrection. True worship is looking at the Cross through the empty tomb. Worship includes remembering what God has done for you. Worship is respect for the holy (respect is to look at and pay attention to) that which has value in your life. Worship can be realized by singing a passionate song, by intercessory prayer, and by a moral lifestyle. Worship can be an individual response to the "worth-ship of God" or by a collective expression by 2 or 3 or by hundreds and thousands: there are no limits to the number included in true worship. Worship becomes a celebration.

CELEBRATION embraces the value of God in life and acknowledges the worth of God in all aspects of life, individually and collectively. True celebration is an expression of agape love (one-way love that is vertical and directed to God). Worship normally includes collect, confession, communion, and celebration. *Collect* is the gathering "together" of assembled believers in unity responding to the pardon and promises of God; this is collective worship. *Confession* is an individual act of admission of our humanity, the acknowledgement of guilt, and the affirmation of forgiveness. *Communion* is for born again believers walking in fellowship with God and others; it includes a sharing of common beliefs and expectations. Communion suggests closeness of relationship and remembrance of the death, burial and resurrection of Christ. True celebration and worship should lead to individual and collective lifestyle witness and outreach for the Gospel.

Expanding the Kingdom through congregational fellowship – *a gathering of kinship groups and friends with common values and interests.*

CONGREGATION (40-120) Fellowship

Congregation is a subset group of 40-120 believers gathered for fellowship and can be identified by family, interest, and closeness. The congregation is an interactive fellowship unit of the assembly celebration where individuals pay attention to those around them and enjoy a shared experience through spiritual fellowship. Congregation is a gathering of like-minded individuals who enjoy association with others through a kind of kinship response normally understood as fellowship. This is a cohesive unit of the celebration that is an expression of Philadelphia-type of "brotherly love." Philia love

Increasing the Kingdom through spiritual conversion –*a personal change in nature, purpose, function or lifestyle: a process not an event.*

CELL (8-12) Personal Evangelism

Anytime an unconverted individual makes it to the sanctuary unsaved it is evident the local program of evangelism is not working. Evangelism is the function of a Christian lifestyle that finds and cultivates individuals and presents the good news of salvation to an informed individual who leads to conversion. The converts are brought into the assembly for identification with the Trinity through Baptism and scriptural instruction in lifestyle as presented in the Word of God.

Cell is a small group (8-12) of individuals who meet regularly for prayer and sharing. Small groups of committed believers meeting regularly for discussions about evangelism can enable individuals to become soul winners. Prospective converts may be invited to the session for exposure to serious believers. Such lifestyle evangelism works in a complicated and confused world, but it must be encouraged. Perhaps the church should replace their committees with Cell groups with agendas for advancing the kingdom.

Personal evangelism is done by converts. Individual converts must grow in grace and knowledge and become a disciple to learn more of Christ before they can become a "sent one" with a message of salvation to others. Thus becoming a witness, a believer develops a lifestyle. Witness comes from the word *martyr* "willing to suffer for a cause." Martyrs of the past were not *martyrs* because they died for their faith; they died for their faith because they lived their faith and were true witnesses or *martyrs*.

True celebration and worship directed toward God and fellowship within a like-minded congregation advances expansion of the kingdom through evangelism. One becomes two; two becomes four; four become sixteen: this is exponential growth. In spiritual development there is an exponential function: the exponent is the work of the Holy Spirit in the life and witness of individual believers supported by a missional church.

Cell Enlargement and Cell Division

The normal growth of living things is perpetuated by cell enlargement and cell division, but the process does not always work effectively or efficiently. There is not always a readiness to grow or the resources to grow normally. In the scientific study of plants there are differences as individual plants adjust to the soil and the environment.

In biology one deals with the science of all forms of life, including their classification, physiology, chemistry, and interactions. This study is concerned with living organisms, their structure, function, growth, origin, abnormalities over time, and reproduction. Abnormalities include size, number, shape, color, and miscellaneous anomalies. The study of plant life includes vitality, survival, and reproductive strength.

In the study of Miller's Living Systems, all living things share commonalities of a specific origin, a pattern of developmental growth, viability, and decline and death. According to Miller, organisms, organizations, and organizations share a similar process. Since the church is considered a social institution, a local church or a collection of churches, would share a similar life-span process. One thing is certain: the process of growth is dynamic and the phases or stage normally relate to the strengthening of the unit for viability and reproduction rather than being related to size.

Enlarging the Kingdom through discipleship training –*making Biblical discipleship a core learning experience.*

CLASS (Infinity #) Discipleship Training

Class is best understood as regular Sunday school groups who meet to study Christian discipleship. A class is of indefinite size, but must be populated by individuals interested in the subject at hand. A pastor should remember that in Acts 11 it took Saul and Barnabas "one whole year" teaching converts before their lifestyle was recognized by a pagan community.

Broadening the Kingdom through an unconventional Christian lifestyle—*living that reflects personal attitudes, way of life, values, and worldview.*

(5) CHRISTIAN LIFESTYLE (Infinity #) Witnessing lifestyle.

During World War II in a Luftwaffe Prison Camp in England that consisted of German airmen, a modern exponential explosion of conversion occurred. From the testimony of a Medical Doctor present, a group of British women decided an act of Christian charity would be to share their bread ration with the German airmen. When half-loafs of bread were placed on the table, the German ranking officer complained to Dr. A. E. Wilder-Smith about the half ration. When he was told about the women sharing their bread ration, it opened his heart to Dr. Wilder-Smith's witness of God's Saving Grace. It is a record of exponential conversion where most of the German inmates of the prisoner of war camp embraced Christian conversion. It is believed that Christian acts of kindness in lifestyle witness can enlarge the kingdom. Perhaps the assembly celebration should produce a daily lifestyle witness that could be expressed as the sweet bread of life or C.A.K.E. –Christian Acts of Kindness Every-day.

Extending the Kingdom through church congregation planting –*establishing a new local Christian congregation.*

CONGREGATION PLANTING (Outreach and Expansion)

Planting new congregations in neighborhoods where there are limited Christian witnesses should be a commitment of all churches. A small congregation of 100 could easily "tithe" ten members to initiate a new assembly in another neighborhood. The same would be true of a 500 member Celebration could "tithe" fifty and a 1,000 member church could "tithe" 100 families to open a new marketplace center for the gospel.

The church has been called God's Garden. What does it take to grow a garden? Diligent cultivation, careful prayerful planting, constant attention, saintly patience.... then it must be touched by the hand of God. A spiritual and exponential assembly is a growing community of leaders committed to accelerating the multiplication of healthy, reproducing faith-based congregations and lifestyle Christian communities.

Take a look at nature: God's plan for growth. A single grain of corn can be multiplied by the simple process of planting and caring for the new plant. God's Eden commandment "Be fruitful and replenish the earth" could easily be understood In terms of obligatory church planting for outreach and expansion of the kingdom.

Developing the Kingdom through missional behavior -- *adopting the thinking, behaviors, and practices of a missionary in order to engage others worldwide with the gospel message.*

CHRISTIAN MISSIONS (globalizing the gospel)

Christian Missions has been defined improperly as home and foreign activity of the church. Missions is not foreign or home; Christian missions is everywhere by everyone at all times. In fact, every believer is a missionary without a Capitol Letter. It is part of the DNA of a convert. Conversion provides a spiritual element that could be called a Divine Nurturing Attribute. A true convert will have the seed of this spiritual DNA and it should grow into active behavior and practices that shares the gospel message to anyone and everyone who will listen. This is Christian missions!

Personal viewpoints and values are major factors that impact the daily struggle of leaders and managers. This is true in all aspects of life, but especially true at the place of work. Most organized enterprises today talk about good business to guide the required effort to achieve a profitable status. However, saying the right words is the easy part; doing the work to make the words happen is the struggle. This is where faith-based principles and values influence the decision and behavior process in organizations.

THE MODIFIED ENGEL'S SCALE MUST BE UNDERSTOOD TO ASSURE COMMUNICATION WITH THE PAGAN POOLS

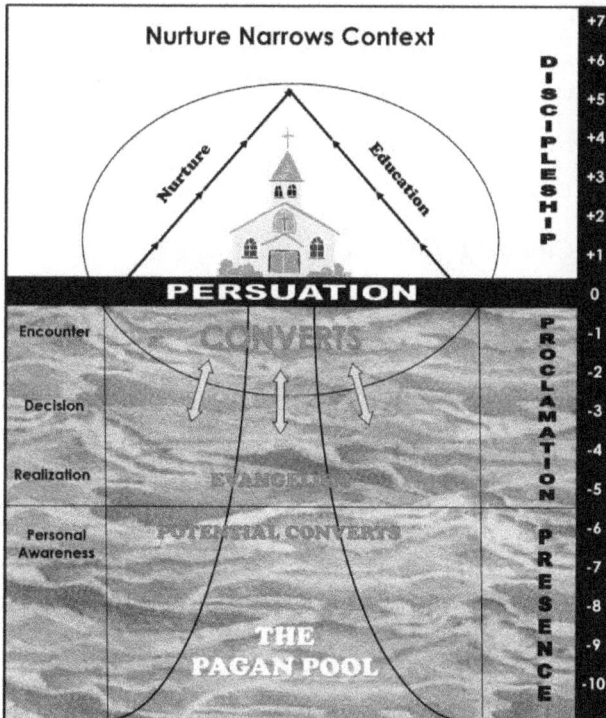

As the church and individual believers reach into the marketplace and the pagan pools for potential converts, a clear contextual analysis is required before intervention strategies can be implemented. Individuals and groups around the world are at different levels of non-awareness and awareness. One must recognize a declining scale to know at which point the person is open to the Gospel. Intervention strategies may be imposed at different levels as individuals and groups move toward acceptance of Christianity:

- Awareness of Supreme Being--10
- No Effective Knowledge of Christianity--9
- Initial Awareness of Need--8
- Interest—Acceptance of Medium--7
- Awareness of Gospel--6
- Grasp of Implications--5
- Positive Attitude--4
- Personal Problem Recognition--3
- Challenge/Decision to Act--2
- Repentance/Faith in Christ--1

Periods of awareness and intervention by Christians are required prior to a direct encounter that may or may not lead to the Making of a Disciple. The periods are:

1. A Period of Awareness (10-6)
2. Realization (5)
3. A Period of Decision (4-2)
4. Encounter (1)

Intervention strategies take three forms:

1. A Ministry of Presence (10-6)

2. A Period of Proclamation (5-2)

3. A Time of Persuasion (1)

Once an Encounter is made during the time of persuasion, the individuals involved must make a firm decision. This decision begins a Period of Incorporation. Converts must be nourished and nurtured through Discipleship Training into the active life of a Christian. Several steps are evident:

1. Post-decision Evaluation

2. Incorporation

3. Personal Fruitfulness

4. Conceptual Growth

5. Discovery of Spiritual Gifts

6. Incarnational (Social) Growth

7. Stewardship

8. Prayer

9. Use of Spiritual Gifts

10. Witness – Reproduction

The Period of Incorporation requires the Christian community to assist the convert in learning to follow Christ. These steps are:

1. Discipleship

2. Christian Education

3. Body Life

4. *Koinonia* (fellowship)

5. *Diakonia* (service)

51. YELLOW APPLES ON A RED APPLE TREE

In the front yard was a small red apple tree, but one of the branches produced an apple yellowish in color. I was curious, so Grandfather explained that the branch producing the yellow apple was grafted into the red apple tree. I was fascinated. How do you do that? How does it work?

With great patience Grandfather explained the process of splitting the branches in a specific way and placing them together. He then showed me about binding them together tightly with twine and covering the whole joint area with bee's wax. He shared that the grafting process was limited because the new branch was a "taker" and not a "giver." Nature nourishes trees with a supply of a watery liquid called sap. It moves upward in part through an intricate supply system. It seems for the most part the grafted branch sucks nourishment from the roots of the host tree, but it doesn't give anything back. Other branches assist the tree through sap-lifting forces created by evaporation and transpiration. This is a kind of breathing water through the leaves. The grafted branch doesn't do this.

The grafted branch uses all the sunshine and rain on its leaves to produce its own yellow apple. It is a strain on the original tree, because the grafted branch actually takes sap away from the other branches bearing red apples. Too many grafts and they would suck the life out of a tree in the process of producing apples.

I learned a lesson about givers and takers and realized that most of us at some time or the other may be on both ends of that stick. Takers should work at giving, and givers should not begrudge their giving. Scripture is clear, "It is more blessed to give than to receive." I understood that a life of ministry was one of giving not taking.

This philosophy has permeated my adult life and assisted my knowledge of church growth, evangelism, and the development of educational institutions. An understanding of the concept of grafting may clarify the problem as it relates to the integration of communities. One does not have to be a horticulturist to see the disadvantage of foliage without fruit or different kinds of fruit growing on the same tree. Such groups become "takers" without giving a fair share commitment to the infrastructure, which forms the basis for their existence.   It's kind of like extended dependence on government; one receives but does not return in taxes.

Scripture in Romans 11 explains a conceited and egotistical perspective, which resulted in "taking without giving." The character of a grafted branch illustrated the idea. Paul said, "You do not support the root, but the root supports you." A grafted branch does not support the root, which nourishes its life, but the root supports the engrafted branch. The grafted branch may live, grow, produce foliage and even fruit, but remains an unorthodox part of the larger unit. It often becomes militant and radical and is a liability to the original unit. The graft may also become a hindrance to growth and fruit bearing by sapping strength from the source. This may explain the advance of denominations at the expense of Christianity.

52. PROTEST VS. CONTROVERSY:
THE PRO AND CON DEBATE

Latin words are the secret to understanding those who protest. The struggle of Protestant Reformers was to reform and move people to follow Sacred Scripture rather than the whims of men. The energy used was to improve not destroy. A prefix of "pro" or "con" are opposite each other; "pro" used as a prefix means advancing or projecting forward and when occurring on words from Latin means "forward." The concept of protestant originates from the Latin word "protestari" meaning "declare publicly, testify for something." The state of prolonged dispute over conflicting opinion is called controversy. This word was coined from two Latin words meaning "turned in an opposite direction" and "against" or "to turn against." A pro-"test" requires a positive assessment of the situation and a constructive outcome. All civil-disobedience must be factually based and structured toward a positive conclusion. In other words, protest should have constructive analysis and assessment, not just censure and disapproval. Protest within a democracy should have a positive agenda with an understanding that "slinging mud is actually losing ground" for the cause at hand. An early truism in philosophy was clear: "one never reaches a positive conclusion beginning with a negative premise."

Whether the desired reform came from Martin Luther or Dr. King, both being devout leaders, the model was non-violent and established a pattern for positive change. When Luther nailed his 95-theses (plan for reform) to the church door in Germany, his effort was to bring positive change to the personal convictions of the German people. He used the proposition, "the just shall live by faith" as an optimistic and constructive strategy to gain positive change. Luther delineated specific entities that were the foundations of faith and the items that should be changed to be in line with sacred scripture. On the other hand, Dr. King was clear that he dreamed of a better day in the American society and that his assessment against injustice and discrimination was not in line with the sacred governmental documents: "We hold these truths to be self-evident: that all men are created equal, that they are endowed by their Creator with certain unalienable rights, that among these are life, liberty, and the pursuit of happiness." In Jefferson's draft the words were "sacred and un-deniable", but Franklin edited the draft to read "self-evident" and it was approved by vote. This is the way Statesmen solve differences – through the voting process not public rebuke or denunciation. All constructive protest must be assessed, evaluated and non-violent.

Perhaps present-day protesters fail to understand the ethics or the philosophy of social change. There must be leadership to control a positive focus; and clear knowledge of how to reform the system or improve a person or party. Just as Luther emphasized spiritual foundations, Dr. King advanced moral, ethical, and Constitutional Foundations. Constitutional Foundations were used in the same way the Reformers of the Middle Ages emphasized the authority of the Sacred Scripture that was above the impulses, frenzies, and rages of a few. Even perceived injustice or disagreement requires clarity and understanding rather than negative controversy. Any and all resistance to policy, personalities, or parties should be based on a valid argument from the founding principles that were preserved in the Constitution. Otherwise, we have lawlessness, riot, and disorder. Built into Constitutional Government are ways and means to present logical protest when there is injustice or oppressive government pressure to behave against sacred principles or the best practices of business and industry.

Ancient sacred writings acknowledged that "God works through the system, when the system works." When Jesus healed the ten (10) men with Leprosy and told them to follow the rules and go to the Temple for certification and relief from their segregation in society, all obeyed, but one, a Samaritan, who returned to thank Jesus. Why did this man behave differently that the nine (9)? He was not a Jew and was not welcome in the Temple. The present system did not work for him so he employed a positive solution by thankfully returning to Jesus. "God works through the system when the system works!" The same is true of Constitutional Government, most of the time it works; when it doesn't work, the answer is the thankful privilege of "voting" by those who feel marginalized, excluded or maltreated. The solution is the constructive action of citizens at the ballot box, not negative rebellion and mayhem on Main Street. Certainly there are times and seasons when individuals, groups, or parties must work outside the existing system to call attention to injustice and make a positive effort to change, improve, or correct the system. This, however, is not an excuse for confusion and pandemonium by a leaderless and bad-mannered gang throwing rocks, burning, stealing or using rudeness and offensive language against those they despise.

53. THE LAST ONES

Born in the 1930s and early 40s, we exist as a special age cohort. We are the "last ones." We are the last, climbing out of the depression, who can remember the winds of war and the war itself with fathers and uncles going off. We are the last to remember ration books for everything from sugar to shoes to stoves. We saved tin foil and poured fat into tin cans. We saw cars up on blocks because tires were not available. We saw milk delivered in a horse drawn cart.

We are the last to hear Roosevelt's radio assurances and to see gold stars in the front windows of our grieving neighbors. We can also remember the parades on August 15, 1945; VJ Day. We saw the "boys" home from the war build their Cape Cod style houses, pouring the cellar, tar papering it over and living there until they could afford the time and money to build the rest of it.

We are the last who spent childhood without television; instead imagining what we heard on the radio. As we all like to brag, with no TV, we spent our childhood "playing outside until the street lights came on." We did play outside and we did play on our own. There was no little league. The lack of television in our early years meant, for most of us, that we had little real understanding of how the world really was. Our Saturday afternoons, if at the movies, gave us newsreels of the war and the holocaust sandwiched in between westerns and cartoons. Newspapers and magazines were written for adults. We are the last who had to find out for ourselves.

As we grew up, the country was exploding with growth. The G.I. Bill gave returning veterans the means to get an education and spurred colleges to grow. VA loans fanned a housing boom. Pent up demand, coupled with new installment payment plans, put factories to work and created jobs. New highways brought jobs and mobility. The veterans joined civic clubs and became active in politics. In the late 40s and early 50's the country seemed to lie in the embrace of brisk but quiet order as it gave birth to its new middle class. Our parents understandably became absorbed with their own new lives. They were free from the confines of the depression and the war. They threw themselves into exploring opportunities they had never imagined. We were not neglected but we were not the all-consuming family focus. They were glad we played outside by ourselves. They were busy discovering the post-war world.

Most of us had no life plan, but with the unexpected virtue of ignorance and an economic rising tide we simply stepped into the world and went to find out. We entered a world of overflowing plenty and opportunity; a world where we were welcomed. Based on our naïve belief that there was more where this came from, we shaped life as we went forward.

We enjoyed a luxury; we felt secure in our future. Of course, just as today, not all Americans shared in this experience. Depression poverty was deep rooted. Polio was still a crippler. The Korean War was a dark presage in the early 50s and by mid-decade school children were ducking under desks. China became Red China. Eisenhower sent the first "advisors" to Vietnam. Castro set up camp in Cuba and Khrushchev came to power.

We are the last to experience an interlude when there were no existential threats to our homeland. We came of age in the late 40s and early 50s. The war was over and the cold war, terrorism, climate change, technological upheaval and perpetual economic insecurity had yet to haunt life with persistent anxiety. Only we can remember both a time of apocalyptic war and a time when the world was secure and full of bright promise and plenty. We fully experienced both.

We grew up at the best possible time, a time when the world was getting better not worse. We are the '"last ones!"
– *Original Author Unknown*

54. MOTHER'S CLOTHESLINE

We are the last generation that will remember the clothes line. Great memories for some of us! It's the poem at the end that's the best! There is one thing that's left out. We had a long wooden pole (clothes pole) that was used to push the clotheslines up so that longer items (sheets/pants/etc.) didn't brush the ground and get dirty. There were even rules for clotheslines:

1. You had to hang the socks by the toes... NOT the top.

2. You hung pants by the BOTTOM/cuffs... NOT the waistbands.

3. You had to WASH the clothesline(s) before hanging any clothes - walk the entire length of each line with a damp cloth around the lines.

4. You had to hang the clothes in a certain order, and always hang "whites" with "whites," and hang them first.

5. You NEVER hung a shirt by the shoulders - always by the tail! What would the neighbors think?

6. Wash day on a Monday! NEVER hang clothes on the weekend, or on Sunday, for Heaven's sake!

7. Hang the sheets and towels on the OUTSIDE lines so you could hide your "unmentionables" in the middle (perverts & busybodies, y'know!)

8. It didn't matter if it was sub-zero weather.... clothes would "freeze-dry." I remember my Grandfather's union suits standing by themselves frozen. How many remember union suits?

9. ALWAYS gather the clothes pins when taking down dry clothes! Pins left on the lines were "tacky"!

10. If you were efficient, you would line the clothes up so that each item did not need two clothes pins, but shared one of the clothes pins with the next washed item.

11. Clothes off of the line before dinner time, neatly folded in the clothes basket, and ready to be ironed. (IRONED? Well, that's a whole OTHER subject!)

55. AND NOW A POEM....

A clothesline was a news forecast,
to neighbors passing by,

There were no secrets you could keep,
when clothes were hung to dry.

It also was a friendly link, for neighbors always knew
When company stopped by to spend a night or two.

For then you'd see the "fancy sheets,"
and towels upon the line;

You'd see the "company table cloths,"
with intricate designs.

The line announced a baby's birth,
from folks who lived inside,

As brand new infant clothes were hung,
so carefully with pride!

The ages of children were known;
by watching the sizes change, you'd know
how much they'd grown!

It also told when illness struck,
as extra sheets were hung;

Then nightclothes and a bathrobe too,
haphazardly were strung.

It also said, "On vacation now,"
when lines hung limp and bare.

It told, "We're back!" when full lines sagged,
with not an inch to spare!

New folks in town were scorned upon,
if wash was dingy and gray,

As neighbors carefully raised their brows,
and looked the other way.

But clotheslines now are of the past,
for dryers make work much less.

Now what goes on inside a home
is anybody's guess!

We really miss that way of life;
it was a friendly sign,

When neighbors knew each other best...
by what hung on the line.

There is no reason to be in the dark. There can be light at the *beginning* of the tunnel.

❖

APPENDIX: A

THINGS LEARNED AND PASSED
TO MY SONS

Some years ago I identified about 300 things learned through the past decades and decided to pass them along to my sons.

1. Working for a good cause may be sufficient compensation and pay becomes a bonus.

2. The rabbit's foot didn't save the rabbit.

3. Honest achievement is a journey; not a stroll in the park.

4. A reasonable man should not attempt to ride a nightmare.

5. Leadership determines direction in an organization.

6. Organization determines accomplishment in an institution.

7. Human resources determine achievement of an enterprise.

8. Confidence determines teamwork on a mission.

9. Leaders see the obvious that others may overlook.

10. Failure is a fundamental part of accomplishment.

11. Success is an insufficient measurement for service; the word is sufficiency.

12. True ministry is not determined by how one earns a living, but by a relationship with God and others.

13. The grocery replaced grandfather's farm and grandmother's garden.

14. Holding on alone is not sufficient to climb the rope.

15. Opinions are useless; observations are necessary.

16. Winning a race with slow runners is no real victory

17. Change is certain; growth is not.

18. Riding a slow horse just to get in the race is laughable.

19. Counsel may be necessary to understand the problem, but action is required to solve it.

20. Constant learning is required to keep up in any field.

21.   Underestimating opposition produces the same results as overestimating yourself.

22.   Nothing is accomplished without the confidence and assistance of others.

23.   Prayer is determined by one's faith not the number of words.

24.   God provided two ears and one mouth to encourage man to listen more.

25.   Homework is required to make the home work.

26.   Nothing is discovered walking on a convenient path.

27.   Satisfaction with status quo is a slippery slope to failure.

28.   Holy discontent is required to do a spiritual work.

29.   Long-range goals are required to avoid short-range disappointments.

30.   Excellence requires continuous effort over time.

31.   Inspiration demands perspiration to achieve.

32.   If God leads, it is not impossible.

33.   Races are won by looking at the goal not at other runners.

34.   The best way to become lost is to follow a crowd.

35. An uncultivated field will never produce a garden.

36. Never attempt to analyze the surface symptoms, look for the real problem.

37. A chain breaks at its weakest link.

38. Christianity has lost its Sunday punch because the first day of the week has become the psychological last day.

39. Complicated programming limits mobilization, because it is not understood.

40. A common cause of stagnation in organizations is over-programming.

41. Sunday is the first day and sets the pace and pattern for the week.

42. A theology of coercion creates wasted attempts to motivate Christians to "go and do"... instead of teaching them to "do as they go."

43. Do not leave the work to chance, spell out the details.

44. Striving to be outstanding in your field may make you as lonely as a scarecrow.

45. Expect a few arrows if you are alone at the top of the ladder.

46. The seated position causes most of mankind's physical ailments.

47. It is foolish to sit on the premises when you could stand on the promises.

48. Eating the seed corn is a sure way to starvation.

49. The fruit of every accomplishment contains seeds that should be planted and cultivated.

50. Mankind concocts all kinds of paraphernalia and programming to cover up weaknesses.

51. Tools must fit the hand of the worker to produce a good product.

52. It takes less electric power to make a noise than it does to burn a light.

53. All true achievement is made within the framework of personal experience.

54. When teachers stop learning they should be forced to stop teaching.

55. If the student did not learn the teacher did not teach.

56. The best way to understand the story facts of the Gospel is to experience the living God personally and share what you learned with others.

57. Only those who have experienced the Truth propagate honest reality.

58. Home should be a safe haven for family and friends.

59. Mankind has no pain that true love cannot touch.

60. Since the Church could be called God's Kitchen where family and friends gather, the kitchen at home should be a sanctuary for all who might enter.

61. Earth has no sorrow that heaven cannot heal.

62. Physical death is the ultimate spiritual healing.

63. Negative goodness alone is not sufficient to meet the standard of a moral life.

64. A recent convert understood the principle of assimilative reading and wrote, "I am reading the Bible and behaving it."

65. Unless words, concepts, and paragraphs explode creatively, revealing life as it is and suggesting changes for the better, reading is a waste of time.

66. The General is still a soldier.

67. One may hear the sound of the sermon and never get the meaning of the message.

68. Why not drop a few activities that are not working and place priority on an action plan.

69. A "Wait till Sunday" attitude will rob you of spiritual vitality.

70. Vital workers are alienated from a good cause by routine activity.

71. Some abuse their sacred trust by attempting to manipulate spiritual growth.

72. Deceptive behavior in the name of religion becomes a camouflage for evil.

73. Machines cannot be substituted for personal effort in a worthy endeavor.

74. Copying techniques or programs without understanding the background and philosophy is as taxidermy is to a live animal.

75. Philosophy determines goals and goals determine methods.

76. Success normally contains the seeds of failure.

77. Material gifts could be an attempt to buy one's way out of personal responsibility.

78. During the Civil War, the rich could pay a bounty and avoid military service.

79. The disbursement of funds in a non-profit enterprise is a sacred trust.

80. Some promotional schemes suggest shallowness in a leader's perception of people and programs.

81. The best results come from a systematic involvement over time.

82. An effort suffers when too few attempt to do too much.

83. The dissemination of information is best accomplished person to person.

84. Leaders must be free to think, plan, and organize while others handle the details.

85.   An effective program must appeal to the drives that produce action: the desire for social approval, the need to be of service, and the wish for God's blessing.

86.   When a task is understood and supervised, it can be accomplished.

87.   Words must be translated into the language of relationship to be effective.

88.   The real challenge of leadership is to motivate the cloistered multitude to participate in a larger cause.

89.   The status quo is much like static in communications; it clouds the senses and numbs the spirit.

90.   The growth of a cause is unlimited when leaders step out on faith and concentrate on a central idea.

91.   An opportunity to do well equals an obligation to act at the moment.

92.   To be effective, the central idea guiding an organization must be shared with anyone who will listen at the earliest point in time, at the greatest distance from the institution.

93.   Never wait to pass a compliment; people actually die everyday.

94.   Upward delegation means someone did not want to assume responsibility.

95. A solution for upward delegation is present action by the first person to discover and identify the problem.

96. Procrastination greatly handicaps any effort to move forward.

97. The technique of the finished task prevents many problems.

98. Idolize only those you know personally. Do not trust the PR image presented by the media talking heads.

99. Assume responsibility for yourself and develop self-sufficiency.

100. In the division of labor, always take your fair share.

101. Always do more that you are asked to do and you will always have a job.

102. Don't get bogged down in nonessentials or unproductive details.

103. It may appear that one is doing the work of others, but in reality one person can only do the work of one person.

104. Only when every worker is daily involved can the work load be properly distributed.

105. A plan coming up from the people works better than one sent down from the top or brought in from outside.

106. An inadequate leader may function better than a qualified individual unwilling to work.

107. Be aware that vested interest often complicates meaningful change.

108. Prestige and positional power does not authorize one to act unfairly.

109. Be cautious in waking a sleeping giant.

110. To manipulate is to get another to do what you want done.

111. To motivate is to assist another in doing what they want to do.

112. Motivation is really "motive" plus "action." One's motive must be understood to recommend an appropriate action.

113. The programming treadmill is really a prison of previous patterns.

114. Changing one's mind does not improve the attitude. Action is required to change one's attitude.

115. Information or facts become knowledge only when they are used to answer a question or solve a problem.

116. Adults learn differently than children.

117. The basic skills of leadership are the ability to sort out the facts, make decisions, and work effectively with people.

118. Ministry is the work of all laity, not the prerogative of a few clergy.

119. Motivation by a change agent is required to encourage most individuals to put forth

the extra effort required to learn new things.

120. An open mind is essential to learning.

121. Filtering out new ideas instead of giving them serious consideration is an adult thing.

122. Learning involves change and most adults resist change because no personal benefit is expected.

123. Leaders must demonstrate solutions rather than simply answer questions.

124. Motivation is the key to learning.

125. Past experience and present data are usually the best tools for problem solving.

126. Adults do not learn by storing information to be used later. They must see a present use for the new material.

127. The learning rates may decline with age, but not the capacity to learn.

128. The aging process is slowed by interest in health, religion, friendship, vocation, politics, aesthetics, economics, and recreation.

129. Action and feeling go together and by regulating action, which is directly controlled by the will, feelings may be indirectly regulated.

130. One, who only officiates, may be classified as simply an officer and not as a leader.

131. Leaders have the ability to influence others to follow them voluntarily toward stated goals.

132. A personal perspective influences prejudice and becomes a hindrance to discovering evidence that could change action, attitude, and feelings toward others.

133. Bad attitudes may be unknowingly reproduced.

134. Outlook is a complex pattern of interlocking attitudes that may not permit a change of component parts. Change requires drastic action; it may be all or nothing.

135. Attitude may be changed by a series of constructive acts systematically directed toward the underlying causes.

136. Caution: Unknowingly one constantly renews old attitudes by present activity.

137. Failure comes from unintentionally reinforcing unwanted attitudes.

138. To change, one needs to understand the whole system of behavior that produces the unwanted attitude.

139. Things that aggravate negative and unwanted attitudes must be systematically purged from the mind by direct action.

140. A positive mindset must be superimposed over a poor attitude to bring about creative and innovative thinking.

141. Creative thought or action builds on individual background and heritage.

142. Leaders filter new ideas through their experience to produce a workable program that actually comes up from the people.

143. A variety of ideas provide vitality for a program.

144. Wholehearted participation requires both understanding and ownership of the ideas supporting a program.

145. Innovation starts with a problem to be solved.

146. Innovative activity may actually disrupt the status quo and open the door for progress.

147. A group may develop an idea, but true creativity begins within the mind of an individual

148. Creative people must be protected from the old system of behavior that has aggravated the problem in the past.

149. Intolerance for new ideas creates a barrier to innovation and change.

150. Including creative people in a group process protects individuals from critics.

151. It is a myth that adults cannot learn.

152. An organization must create an open-ended and unstructured environment,

conducive to creative thought, to bring about renewal and growth.

153. Creative juices cannot flow in a proscribed atmosphere.

154. The creative process cannot be rushed or controlled; it is a dynamic force that oprates spasmodically and never methodically.

155. Normally, a creative person maintains a freshness of perception and an unspoiled awareness of life.

156. The absentminded professor is an example of a creative person who heightens awareness of one aspect of life by ignoring other aspects.

157. A creative person may be independent but is normally able to be flexible and find order in experience.

158. There is no shortage of new ideas, just workable ones.

159. A kind of social shock therapy may be needed to create awareness that change is needed.

160. Most organizations suffer from inertia and either remains inactive or continues to move in the same direction.

161. Creative people are easily discouraged when others resist their ideas.

162. Creativity has a tendency to leave some ragged edges.

163. The missing link in failed programs is grass-root participation.

164. Achievement often begins with dissatisfaction.

165. A pioneer is effective with inadequate resources.

166. Just as each spoke in a wagon wheel is equally important, so is each individual in any group.

167. Use all the brains you have and borrow all you can from others.

168. When creative thoughts do not come, hitchhike on the ideas of others.

169. Listening is a process of focusing on what is actually said and meant.

170. Hearing and listening are not the same thing.

171. When one truly listens, action follows.

172. Listening is not remembering, but understanding what is said that is remembered.

173. The brain is the body's superstar that imagines, judges, decides, reviews, and remembers 10,000 facts and identifies the one that matters at the moment.

174. The brain stores sensations and impressions for instant recall and never sleeps.

175. Spontaneity is possible when one is not inhibited or constricted by personal self-interest.

176. The religions of pagan society give mankind no hope.

177. Christ is the ultimate standard by which one should be measured.

178. Man at his best is far enough from truth to be in gross error.

179. Be careful that the light you follow is not the twilight of the evening instead of the Morning Star.

180. Those who keep the faith are not disappointed.

181. Beneath despair is the slumbering force of indestructible hope waiting to be released.

182. With the Incarnation it was no longer necessary for mankind to remain depraved.

183. The Star of Bethlehem brought the dawn of hope to wise men who felt constrained to search for and to worship the Christ-child.

184. Discipline is a system of rules affecting conduct that implies instruction, correction, and training that molds, strengthens, and improves character.

185. Christianity brought a positive message lacking in other religious teachings.

186. Love produces upright and honest conduct.

187. Motive alone gives moral quality to action.

188. The heart, as the seat of virtue and the spring of right conduct, affirms the inward force for moral law.

189. Simplicity is a quality of religion and discernment in the moral life.

190. Love, sympathy, and forgiveness are essential elements of a moral life.

191. Faith, love, and hope are the essential elements of the Christian life.

192. Telling a story is a good way to illustrate the truth.

193. An economy of words is a blessing to all.

194. Good character produces influence.

195. Strongly worded principles are practical guides to daily life.

196. Individual narrowing occurs as people age and eliminate things they do poorly; consequently, a narrow view of life is developed and individuals are satisfied to walk on a narrow path or sit in a straitjacket of complicated programs.

197. The moral dynamics of love can transform external conformity into a manifesto of ethical conduct.

198. Jesus took 613 laws and transformed
      them into the Law of Love that extended
      to both neighbor and enemy.

199. An evil eye offends the heart and makes it
      guilty of immorality.

200. Character should be unquestionable,
      making an oath unnecessary.

201. Life is essentially dialogue; no one can live
      or die to himself.

202. Each individual must relate to a significant
      other to be complete.

203. Never fight with obnoxious people; they
      have nothing to lose.

204. Always listen to the needs of others; even
      those unspoken.

205. Keep every encounter positive.

206. Resolve to be tender with the young,
      compassionate with the aged,
      sympathetic with the striving, and tolerant
      of the weak and the wrong. Sometime in
      your life you will have been all of these.

207. One cannot deal with error unless the
      truth is known.

208. Spontaneous activity is good for the soul.

209. Never give up what you have gained.

210. Zeal should be directed toward a
      productive life not personal enjoyment.

211. One obstacle to the moral life is the misconception that spirituality is reserved for others.

212. Never procrastinate. How will you find time tomorrow to do those things left undone today?

213. If there is not enough time to do it right, how will you find time to do it over?

214. When you have your mind or hand on the problem - fix it!

215. A transformation within compels one to share the good news.

216. Based on emphasis by proportion, God intended the writings of Luke and Paul to be given extra consideration since each wrote about one-fourth of the New Testament.

217. An apology is the first step in correcting a broken relationship.

218. Sidetracks usually become a dead end.

219. When you sling mud, you are losing ground.

220. Sarcasm normally raises the heat without shedding light on the issues.

221. Never walk blindfolded down a path at the direction of others.

222. Reframe criticism; you may discover the person cares for you.

223. Two are required to make a contract; one can break it.

224. Purpose declares a general direction and is always singular. One can never go in two directions at a time.

225. When one says "purposes," they usually mean objectives or reasons.

226. A purpose may be multifaceted and may be divided into two or more objectives.

227. A single objective restates the purpose, but as a subset should never stand-alone. There must be two or more.

228. A single goal restates an objective, but, as a subset should never stand-alone.

229. A goal requires multiple standards or criteria to determine achievement.

230. Leadership is the ability to influence others to follow you voluntarily toward stated goals.

231. The willingness to accept assigned tasks is a mark of maturity.

232. No one should be satisfied with his/her spiritual state.

233. History reveals that devastation follows the corruption of truth.

234. Compromise means "with – promise" and becomes a contract or agreement to assist two parties to move forward.

235. The Bible means exactly and only what the first hearers understood it to say.

236. Most of what one says is understood or validated by nonverbal means.

237. Beware of people who are insincere, selfish, lustful, divisive, and absent of compassion.

238. One can easily become imprisoned by previous patterns.

239. Busyness produces a treadmill syndrome that limits productive activity.

240. Salvation separates one from sins - not friends.

241. As you climb the Hill of Difficulty, don't forget your R.O.P.E. (Rely On Prayer Everyday)

242. There is no responsibility without full accountability.

243. Bigger is not necessarily better. Remember the Titanic.

244. The social fabric of America is complicated and one must work to make moral values viable in a pluralistic society.

245. Prudence without action will never produce achievement in any endeavor.

246. The Bible is a relational book; it is more about attitudes to be caught than about doctrines to be taught.

247. One should realize that the world is viewed through a personal cultural perspective.

248. Never invest in property alone; people also appreciate in value.

249. Mobility of society has produced complex relationships. Once communities were filled with family and friends; now they have become a gathering of strangers.

250. When a way out cannot be found to a difficulty, learn to manage your life around it.

251. Friends are better than money in the bank. One may spend the "interest" without decreasing the principle

252. Waging peace is a long crusade.

253. Victory is a short lived event and the armed forces need more reward than just victory.

254. It is difficult to be broadminded and walk the narrow way.

255. Always take note of the strength an enemy attributes to you; it may be more useful than the opinion of friends.

256. The greatest contribution of family and friends is memories.

257. Experience is more important than education in many fields.

258. Money invested in education is lost unless the student uses what is learned.

259. The idea of knowledge for knowledge sake was the brainchild of a cloistered academic and may not be relevant today or worth remembering.

260. Mature people see the world differently than the other kind of people.

261. Information and data become knowledge only when facts are used to answer a question or solve a problem.

262. Your world view determines the way you treat the environment.

263. Life is best when one lives as if each day were their last day on earth.

264. Erosions of influence are similar to a landslide and extremely hard to stop.

265. Never retire! If you get tired doing nothing you can't stop and rest. Could that be why old people die?

266. One must persevere in a race to get a second wind and reach the finish line.

267. One normally sees family culture as better or best and may be prone to fault others unfairly.

268. It may be better to invest in your children than play the stock market.

269. When you feel that no one cares, call a big company and listen to the recorded message, "Your call is important to us!"

270. No matter how many birds you watch you will never find the little one that told your mother everything you did.

271. How would you feel if the "gold" at the end of the rainbow were green stamps?

272. Every disadvantage can provide a means to rise above circumstances.

273. Credit can become the means to live beyond your earnings.

274. A stopped clock may be right twice a day but that is no reason to keep it around.

275. Bad habits can be replaced through constructive behavior over time.

276. Since most accidents happen within 25-miles of home, moving to another place will not increase your safety.

277. If safety takes second place you could lose the important race of life.

278. A few sensible changes in lifestyle may lengthen your lifeline.

279. The first ten years of marriage are the hardest unless you have been married fifteen or twenty years.

280. People with bifocal glasses may see things you never see.

281. Balance may be the most important ingredient in a triumphant life.

282. Don't meditate for hours searching for inner peace, just do an honest days work.

283. To rekindle an old flame may require a match made in heaven.

284. Passion can become heavy baggage unless shared with a significant other.

285. No one wants to get old until he does and then he wants to get as old as he can.

286. A good barber can usually cut your hair while you wait.

287. A hero's unexpected behavior surprises everyone including the hero.

288. If you are caught between the devil and the deep blue sea, look up for your deliverance, don't try to swim.

289. Don't be suspicious of happiness - enjoy it fully.

290. When your ship comes in try not to be at the airport.

291. Embrace life and living or you will miss lots of fun.

292. Shasta is a good name for a car because she has to have gas, she has to have oil, and she has to have water.

293. Don't be an agnostic - when you die you'll have no where to go.

294. Before you hang up on a telemarketing person ask for their home phone number and promise to call them back.

295. Be a problem-solver, don't worry about making money.

296. The brain is the original search engine, use it regularly and wisely.

297. A trailblazer usually has rough hands or blisters.

298. When you look in a mirror always see a compelling portrait of an important person.

299. If designer babies had been available to your parents, they would have ordered one just like you.

300. Understanding roots is important, but one must never become imprisoned by the patterns of previous generations.

301. One can easily improve their face value with a simple smile.

302. Fear is a good teacher.

303. Work is a privilege.

304. Personality is the only garment most people see.

305. A winning season is accomplished by patient   endurance.

306. Peace of mind and a grudge are mutually exclusive.

307. Always remember - Mothers are miracle workers.

308. Parents may see beauty, but others see only actions.

309. Sharing a few things with others is better than having lots of stuff alone.

310. Spoken words may be lost, but those written remain to speak another day.

311. Evil never attacks your past or present; evil forces work against your future.

312. Let negatives be implied, but clearly state the positive.

313. People are brought together for the benefit of both.

314. Listen to others and learn.

315. One can see more clearly how to walk when they look up.

316. When your out-go is more than the income, up-keep will be your down fall.

317. A pencil has an eraser because mistakes happen.

318. Obstacles may alter your path, but should never change your direction.

319. Patience and love are never wasted.

320. Doing good without expecting repayment can make a day perfect.

321. True love directed toward a significant other is life's greatest force for good.

322. A recipe is made to follow not just copy for someone else to do.

323. To be connected is to be part of a relationship chain that links you to others.

324. A child can open the window of your soul and let the light shine into your heart.

325. People who say "I can't" never do; those who say "I can" get things done.

326. Spirituality promises something good in every situation.

327. Since there is a Master Plan, hold on to the   meaning of each moment – good or bad.

328. If trouble comes, and surely it will, remember God has confidence in you... nothing will happen that you and God together can't handle.

329. It is the busy person that always has time to help others.

330. Time is worth more than money; time translates into life...money means things.

331. Progress is not always good: a ball point pen doesn't have an eraser.

332. Age is not measured by body strength, but by clear headed thoughts.

333. Contentment is great gain regardless of what you do, whom you love or where you are.

334. Searching for answers is part of the learning process.

APPENDIX: B

THINGS LEARNED ABOUT ORGANIZATIONAL LIFE

Never Ride A Dead Horse

The tribal wisdom of the Dakota Indians passed on from generation to generation said, *"When you discover that you are riding a dead horse, the best strategy is to dismount and get a different horse."* However, in government, education, and corporate America (Yes, even in nonprofit organizations, more advanced strategies are often employed), such as:

Buying a stronger whip; changing riders; appointing a committee to study the horse; arranging to visit other countries to see how other cultures ride dead horses; lowering the standards so that dead horses can be included; reclassifying the dead horse as living impaired; hiring outside contractors to ride the dead horses; harnessing several dead horses together to increase power and speed; providing additional funding and/or training to increase the dead horse's performance.

Doing a productivity study to see if lighter riders would improve the dead horse's performance; declaring that as the dead horse does not have to eat, it is less costly, carries lower overhead and therefore contributes substantially more to the bottom line of the economy than do some other horses; rewriting the expected performance requirements for all horses based on the performance of dead horses.

And, of course, promoting the dead horse rider to a supervisory position with a raise in pay and increased retirement benefits. Oh, I forgot...and a bigger stable in the new barn for the dead horse.

~

Wisdom does not come packaged in extraordinary people; it is always in the average person who uses common sense.

ABOUT THE AUTHOR

Hollis L. Green, ThD, PhD, DLitt, is a Clergy-Educator with public relations and business credentials and doctorates in theology, education, and philosophy. A Distinguished Professor of Education and Social Change at the graduate level for over three decades, Dr. Green is a Diplomate in the Oxford Society of Scholars, and author of 50+ books and numerous articles. He served six years as a member of the U.S. Senate Business Advisory Board and with certified membership in several public relations societies (RPRC, PRSA, and IPRC). He served pastorates in five states, was a denominational official for 18 years, and traveled in ministry and lectured in over 100 countries.

Dr. Green was the founder of Associated Institutional Developers (A.I.D. Ltd.), (1974) an international Public Relations and Corporate Consultant Company. He was Vice-President of Luther Rice Seminary, 1974-1979, (www.lutherrice.edu), and became the founding President (1981) and Chancellor (1991-2008) and Chancellor, Emeritus of Oxford Graduate School, (www.ogs.edu) As part of a global outreach, Dr. Green founded OASIS UNIVERSITY (2002) in Trinidad, W.I. (www.oasisgradedu.org) where he continues to lecture and teach and assist the administration as Chancellor. Dr. Green also serves as

Secretary-General for the Board of Governors of the Society of Scholars.

In 2004, he assisted in establishing Greenleaf Global Educational Foundation in Colorado to advance issues related to the current needs of society. In addition to his other endeavors, Dr. Green launched GlobalEdAdvance Press (2007) to advance higher education and social change through publishing, curriculum development, instruction, library/learning resources, and global book distribution with 30,000 distributors in 100 countries. His books and assisting authors in publishing are a logical outgrowth of a fifty-year ministry through education. He serves the Author Publisher Partnership PRESS as Corporate Chair and Co-publisher with his son, Barton. Dr. Green continues to travel, speak, teach, write books and work with authors in publishing.

GreenWine Family Books™

A division of

GlobalEdAdvancePress

www.gea-books.com